Albion decided quite early to concentrate on commercials, so there are two vans and a bus on this early Scottish Motor Show stand. The 32hp model that formed the chassis of the bus had been introduced in 1910. *Author's Collection*

British Buses Before 1945

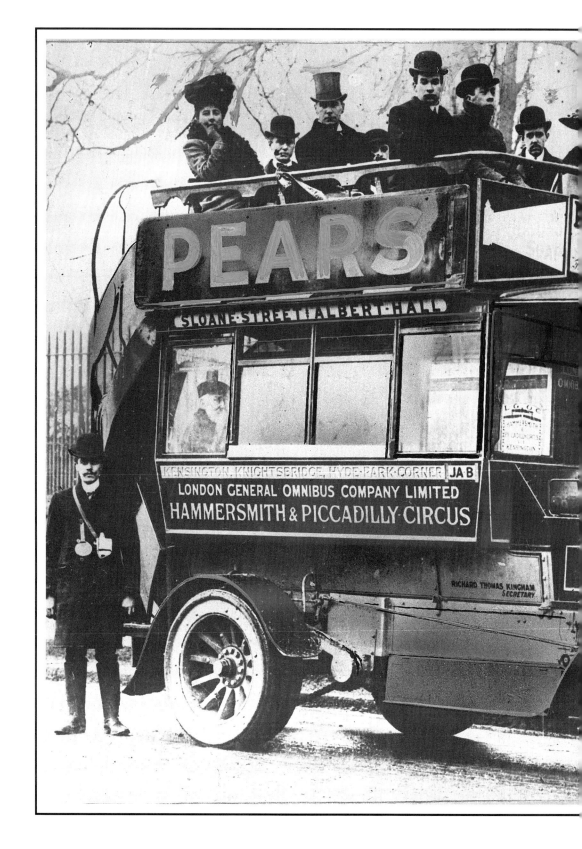

British Buses Before 1945

John Aldridge

IAN ALLAN Publishing

Contents

First published 1995

ISBN 0 7110 2279 8

© Ian Allan Ltd 1995

Published by Ian Allan Publishing

an imprint of Ian Allan Ltd, Terminal House, Station Approach, Shepperton, Surrey TW17 8AS.
Printed by Ian Allan Printing Ltd, Coombelands House, Coombelands Lane, Addlestone, Weybridge, Surrey KT15 1HY.

Front Cover:
The London Transport Museum's preserved LT165 pictured in wartime condition. *LTM*

Half title:
By the late 1920s or early 1930s most buses were reliable and durable. This 1934 Dennis Lancet (*left*) lasted until 1957, and the 1926 Leyland Lion until 1955; both are seen in their later days with Jersey Motor Transport. *Clifford Walters*

Title page:
Some early motorbuses carried adapted bodies off horsebuses, as on this 1905 Swiss Orion, one of two the LGOC put into service. *Author's Collection*

Foreword

There was a wealth of colour and variety in the buses on our roads from the turn of the century. Some 175 different makes of bus, coach or charabanc operated in the UK at some time between 1900 and 1945. Some makers produced, literally, just one vehicle. Many pioneer makers, like many pioneer bus operators, soon fell by the wayside, but others prospered and became almost household names.

At times a lack of foresight, or of advancement among the UK builders, encouraged an influx of European and North American makes. At other times the balance was redressed by British makers winning considerable export business.

In a potted history such as this, it is impossible to more than scratch the surface of what was once a large industry. Books have been written about individual makes, and even about individual models of one make. I have tried to provide interesting, but brief, portraits of some 175 makes which once ran on our roads, and also to mention some of the operators who ran them. One can only marvel at a small make such as Durham Churchill, built in penny numbers in Sheffield, achieving sales in the north of Scotland and

the south of England. And how could a make with such an excellent pedigree as Milnes-Daimler, which once had the lion's share of the market, lose interest and sales just because its selling organisation found it easier or more profitable to sell cars?

Many of the early services were worked by wagonettes, which were little more than cars with extra seats. They were not able to carry enough passengers to make the services they ran profitable, and soon faded from the scene. So I have touched on them only briefly, as they never became part of the mainstream bus story.

Many of the changes that came about, as the result of technical developments or legislation, were applicable to many or most makes, and these are covered in the introduction, rather than reported and repeated under each individual make. The pictures, more than 200 of them, almost tell their own story. Incredible variety, sometimes, from one small maker; surprising uniformity from another.

John Aldridge
November 1994

The rival to the Leyland Titan was the AEC Regent, which was also designed by G. J. Rackham. The unusual 'camel's hump' in the roof was a shortlived feature to keep height down without infringing Leyland patents. These two Short Bros-bodied Regents were operated by Cornish Buses, a company later swallowed by Western National. *Ian Allan Library*

Introduction

'A vehicle without horses and without steam power... the driver of which need not be a mechanic...' wrote the *Financial Times* more than 100 years ago. It was describing a trial run in London, in 1889, of Radcliffe Ward's 'large and rather cumbrous' electric omnibus. But like so many other experiments and trials, it was to come to nothing. Certainly, by the end of the 19th century, among thinking horsebus proprietors, entrepreneurs and inventors there was the firm idea that the time was ripe for development of some kind of mechanical replacement for the horsebus. Just how uncertain it all was is exemplified by the London Steam Omnibus Co, which in 1899 changed its name to the Motor Traction Co. The company was said to have run a one-day trial of a mechanically-propelled bus between Oxford Circus and Ealing, although one report described it as an electric bus. Under its new name the company began the first regular motorbus service in London in October 1899, and that vehicle was certainly petrol-engined. The service lasted just 14 months.

The suggestion in that quotation from the *Financial Times* that the driver need not be a mechanic was not true of the early motorbus. It was not possible to recruit many drivers who had any mechanical ability, but mechanical sympathy was certainly desirable. Later, when numbers of buses were regularly at work on London's streets, one major operator employed roving mechanics to patrol the routes; when one came upon a broken-down bus he would take over, hopefully making some sort of temporary repair that would enable him to get the bus back to the depot.

Events in London in the early days were fairly well chronicled but early buses and bus services elsewhere were not always so well reported. There is also the problem as to what constituted a bus. Some of the early motor vehicles had a space behind the front seats that could be fitted with inward-looking bench seats on each side for a total of six, eight or even more people. These were known as wagonettes and were often used to provide some kind of mechanically-propelled public service.

The Edinburgh Autocar Co began what is thought to be the first licensed urban service in May 1898, using Daimler and MMC wagonettes which cost between £330 and £400. The service lasted until July 1901, when it folded with an accumulated deficit of £14,000. Heavy maintenance costs and the inability to carry sufficient passengers to generate a reasonable return contributed to the failure. There were other ventures in 1898 or 1899 at a wide spread of places, including Clacton, Falkirk, Folkestone, Herne Bay, Llandudno, Mansfield, Mablethorpe, Torquay and Tunbridge Wells. In London the South Western Motor Car Co started a Clapham Junction-Balham-Streatham service with 10-seat Daimler wagonettes in April 1901. High maintenance costs killed it off after a few months, but the service was noteworthy in having been managed by Walter Flexman French, who was later involved with East Kent, Maidstone & District and Southdown. A longer-lived London wagonette service began in September 1901 between Piccadilly Circus and Putney. This was operated by Francis John Bell, who was said to have successfully run motorbuses at Bournemouth for the previous two years. In London he used seven MMC wagonettes carrying six passengers 'inside' and two 'outside', the term 'outside' at that time being used by the Metropolitan Police to describe seats alongside the driver, outside the main saloon. The Police had juris-

Left:
In 1900 the Dundee Motor Omnibus Co took delivery of this steam vehicle supplied by the Lancashire Steam Motor Co. The latter company was later to become Leyland. John Stirling of Hamilton is said to have arranged the sale; later he built the first Stirling and then Scott-Stirling buses. *Author's Collection*

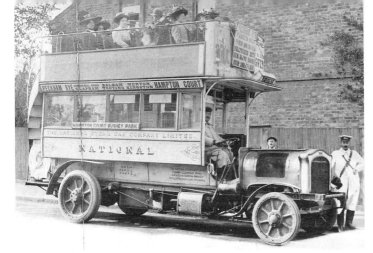

Left:
Clarkson soon developed his steam
buses into quite advanced vehicles;
they boasted dynamo-driven interior lighting for example. The crew
of this one, in Clarkson's own
National fleet, are wearing summer
uniforms. *Author's Collection*

Below:
In the early days wagonettes often
operated passenger-carrying
services, but limited capacity made
their economics doubtful. This
Wolseley-Siddeley dates from
1907. *Author's Collection*

diction over bus operations in London for many years.
Bell's wagonettes had rear-entrance open bodies to
which roofs and sides were added in inclement
weather. Wagonettes soon faded from the scene,
being replaced by more substantial (though not
always more successful) vehicles. Relatively small
vehicles, by the standards of the day, again reappeared in quantity in the mid-1920s. They were 14 to
16-seaters, on pneumatic tyres, when a quirk of the
legislation permitted them to go faster than the more
ponderous and conventional larger buses. But they
were, like the wagonettes, relatively shortlived.

In the early 1900s, even the more substantial vehi-
cles were not always successful. The Birmingham &
Midland Motor Omnibus Co, better known as
Midland Red, was formed in 1904 to take over and
develop services begun by the Birmingham Motor
Express Co in 1903. The fleet was increased, some

older vehicles being replaced, and then in late 1907
the whole fleet was withdrawn (and transferred to
Deal and Warwick) and replaced with horsebuses.
The company had done its best to improve the vehicles; some at least of the Milnes-Daimlers in the fleet,
for example, had their original rack-and-pinion drive
to the rear axle replaced by chain drive. Yet Milnes-
Daimlers were arguably one of the better-designed
makes.

Midland Red was not the only operator to revert to
horses. Nottingham Corporation began a service in
1906 with three open-top Thornycrofts, but gave up in
1909 and substituted horsebuses on the route. That
ceased in 1910, and Nottingham did not resume using
motorbuses until 1920, whereas Midland Red
restarted in 1912. Both Birmingham and Nottingham
had efficient electric tram services, and that could be
one reason for the cessation of these early motorbus

Above:
The Great Western Railway was a pioneer of early motorbus operation, and the Milnes-Daimler was one of the most successful chassis. This example was new in 1905 to an early Devon operator, South Hams Motor Carriers, which was later bought by the GWR. The bus is seen working from Stourbridge. *Author's Collection*

services. In contrast, political decisions had left much of central London without trams but with a dense network of horsebus routes and, along with the huge and growing population and perhaps the prestige of serving the capital, this led to many more operators and makers attempting to serve it.

There were two main factors inhibiting the early development of the motor vehicle in Britain. One was the attitude of the establishment, which was generally against the early motor vehicle. Government in general, the church (then more powerful), magistrates and councils saw no need or use for mechanically-propelled vehicles. Almost the only people interested in owning motorcars were the wealthy young, a very small section of the community. In contrast, continental attitudes were different, particularly in France and Germany. So, despite its engineering abilities and talents, the UK initially possessed very few manufacturers, and most early vehicles were imported.

The other factor was the plateau of development that the horsebus had reached. Its timber structure had been fine-tuned to combine low weight with durability. Many of the earliest motorbuses combined high weight with low capacity. Horsebus proprietors who wanted change effectively wanted a vehicle that would run an all-day service without the need for

several changes of horses. At its height the London General Omnibus Co had a total of 1,418 horsebuses and 17,000 horses. The companies needed stables for the horses, enormous supplies of food and bedding, and vets. Horsebuses usually seated a total of 26 passengers, 14 of them on the upper deck. A pair of horses could work for some three hours before being replaced, and an average horsebus on urban work would run some 65 miles a day, but needed 10 horses, plus extra spare horses to cover illness. Early motorbuses might be able to double that mileage in theory at least, and could carry 34 passengers. Of course, the motorbus cost more to buy, but if you take into account the cost of 10 horses, there was not a big difference in total costs. A rule of thumb, later, was that three horsebuses could be replaced by two motorbuses, allowing for the slightly higher average speed of the motorbus. But on more rural work, where daily mileage was lower, and therefore fewer horses would be needed, the figures were less favourable to the motorbus.

Indirectly the railways also played an important role in the development of the motorbus. They had encouraged the urbanisation of the countryside and provided a coarse passenger-carrying network across the whole country. This, and the rising population, led to the growth of towns and cities and the development of tramway networks in many. By the turn of the century, most tramways were being electrified or were soon to be. But housing was continuing to spread, certainly away from railway stations and lines, and often away from the tram routes too.

Fixed rail transport of any kind is expensive to install and needs a relatively high level of usage to service its fixed costs. Yet there was still considerable local pressure on railways for the construction of further lines. So it is perhaps not surprising that several railway companies were very early operators of motorbuses. Some became quite big operators, with two, the Great Western and North Eastern, quickly building up sizeable fleets, seeing buses as feeders to their networks and as a way of deflecting demand for new railway lines. In the late 1920s and early 1930s the four main railways sold their vehicles and services to existing large operators (or occasionally created new operators) and then took a stake in these bus companies. By this time the railways had realised that the bus and the express coach were threatening much of their traffic.

The GWR began running two Milnes-Daimler single-deckers between Helston station and the Lizard in August 1903, and a month later the NER started a route between Beverley and Leven using new Stirling single-deckers. There were already Light Railway Orders for railways to be built to serve these places, but both companies delayed building because of the high cost and likely low returns. The GWR went on to become the best known and most successful railway bus operator with a fleet of some 300 by the late 1920s. Its first two buses, incidentally, were not new, but had been bought from Sir George Newnes, who had run them in conjunction with his Lynton & Barnstaple Railway. Within a couple of months of starting its Lizard service — in October 1903 to be

precise — the GWR had responded to an offer from Milnes-Daimler to buy 25 new bodied buses for a total cost of £19,541. It must have been the largest-ever order for motorbuses at that time and it contrasted dramatically with the position in London where, at the beginning of 1905, there were still only 20 motorbuses altogether; five of these were also Milnes-Daimlers. But during 1904 in London Thomas Tilling had ordered 24 more Milnes-Daimlers, to augment the one existing in the fleet, though when delivered, not all were used as buses. The following month, the Motor Omnibus Trust — better known as Vanguard — ordered 25 Milnes-Daimlers, with an option on a further 75. The summer of 1904 saw the GWR quick off the mark in another direction, this time with two circular tours from Penzance station. The same year also saw it start the first of several services from Slough station. By the end of 1904 the GWR had 34 motorbuses, the largest fleet in Britain.

No mention of the very early days would be complete without reference to Eastbourne Corporation. It began motorbus operations in April

Below:
Tiered seating was popular on early charabancs, such as this 1908 Leyland, which was supplied to Swiftsure Motors of Clacton-on-Sea. After working there for some time it is said to have returned to Leyland and been exported to the Canary Isles. *Author's Collection*

1903, with a Milnes-Daimler single-decker running to Meads Village, but it was not the first municipal operator. That honour goes to Southampton, which began with an MMC Granville on trial in 1900, and in 1901 put a 12-seater Daimler wagonette into regular service. But that operation was subsequently abandoned, leaving Eastbourne as the earliest municipal operator that has continued unbroken up to the present day. Another early motorbus operator still operating today — albeit under a different name — was the Bristol Tramways & Carriage Co, which started with 12 open-top Thornycroft double-deckers in January 1906, and went on to add Fiat double-deckers and an Arrol-Johnston single-decker to its fleet in the same year. Two years later Bristol started building its own buses on an experimental basis, before going into full production in 1913.

The spur to virtually all development of the motor vehicle in the UK was, of course, the 1896 Highways Act, which abolished most of the infamous provisions of the 1865 Locomotives Act, including the need for a man with a red flag to walk in front of a mechanically-propelled vehicle. The Act of 1896 is still commemorated by the annual London-Brighton veteran car run, in which the newest vehicles date from 1904. Anyone who has seen it will have been amazed at the huge variations in shape, size and mechanism of the cars. So it was with the early motorbus. However, by 1905 a more or less standard shape and form of urban bus had emerged. The first example was said to have been a Milnes-Daimler double-decker with the engine at the front over the front axle, driver behind it, a straight frame and a rear entrance, rear staircase open-top body with a total seating capacity of 34. It was exhibited at the Crystal Palace Motor Car Show in 1904.

But it was to be some years before that relatively simple layout was developed into a reliable and economic vehicle. Chassis frames sagged, axles broke, rigid attachment of engines and gearboxes to the chassis frames resulted in thousands of breakages of bearer arms, and the individual machining of most parts meant that replacement parts rarely fitted. Use of common mild steel for parts that had to be machined and heat-treated caused endless problems; even gears were often made of mild steel which was just case-hardened. These mechanical uncertainties and frailties meant that, at least for urban use, only a double-decker was likely to make money for its operator, and even that was problematical. Lack of profit certainly drove the three major London bus operators to merge in 1908, when the London General, London Road Car and Vanguard fleets all came under one ownership, that of the London General. Between them they owned 885 of the 1,066 motorbuses running in London. There might have been no trams in central London, but there was a new competitor in the shape of the tube railways, which by this time were also loss-making.

Development of the bus in London, then, was slow at best, and its growth slower than elsewhere; horse-buses outnumbered motorbuses in London until 31 October 1910, when there were exactly 1,142 of each type licensed. Even in those days London's traffic was heavy and congested, and frequent stops and starts were hard on primitive and heavy vehicles. London was not alone among capital cities in being apparently backward; Berlin had no motorbuses in 1904.

The merger of the three major London bus operators did not initially help the finances. A special board meeting of the LGOC in 1909 described the great numbers of breakdowns and large sums spent on maintenance as 'enormous and disquieting' and talked of bringing in 'some well-known engineer... say the chief engineer of one of the leading railway companies'. That would have been a strange decision, since such a man would have been an expert on steam propulsion. Perhaps this is how the LGOC's own engineer, Frank Searle, persuaded the company to use the former Vanguard overhaul works at Walthamstow to build its own prototypes. Known as the 'X'-type, it cribbed shamelessly from the best features from the 28 types of vehicle in the existing fleet. Contemporary writers unkindly referred to it as the 'Daimler-Wolseley-Straker type'. After 61 had been built, the LGOC went on to design its famous 'B'-type. Unwittingly the 'B'-type benefited from a decision of the Metropolitan Police to reduce the maximum unladen weight of a bus from the current 5 tons to just 3^1/2 tons. That sent every bus maker with aspirations to sell vehicles for London back to the drawing board. Nobody had military use in mind when the 'B'-type was designed, but it, and mildly modified variants, were to prove of enormous worth in World War 1 — as lorries as well as buses.

The 'B'-type was not alone in this. One of the oldest manufacturers was Leyland, which had begun in 1896 as the Lancashire Steam Motor Co. It produced petrol-engined buses for London in 1905 and also produced huge numbers of vehicles for use in World War 1. Thornycroft was another pioneer maker to produce in quantity for the war effort. The concentration on military vehicles by some of the bus builders led to the brief entry into the market of a few manufacturers who had previously made only goods vehicles, though there was virtually no difference between a chassis for passenger carrying or one for goods.

A different approach to the vexed problems of clutch and transmission and high maintenance costs was taken by Thomas Tilling. Its engineer and manager, Percy Frost Smith, thought difficulties with the gearbox were the main snag, and these were both mechanical and human, the latter being the difficulty in finding suitable drivers who could handle the vehicles proficiently. Drivers were usually selected from horsebus or horse dray drivers, because of their

experience of driving in traffic, but sympathy with, or feeling for, animals did not often translate into mechanical sympathy.

Tilling's first experiment went on the road in 1908, using a Hallford chassis with petrol-electric equipment devised by W. A. Stevens, a Maidstone motor engineer. Known as the SB&S bus, and called 'Queenie' by the crews because of its smoothness, its petrol engine drove a dynamo which fed the current to two electric motors, one driving each rear wheel. An improved version was sold as the Hallford-Stevens, but Tilling took none. Instead, Frost Smith designed the Tilling-Stevens TTA1, which first appeared in 1911. This time the petrol engine and dc generator powered one electric motor which drove a live rear axle. Constraints on Tilling's London operation encouraged it to expand elsewhere, and in 1912 it transferred production of TTA1s to Maidstone, under the aegis of a new company, Tilling-Stevens, in which it had a shareholding. The design soon proved attractive to other operators, Midland Red being the first customer. The battery-electric was another type of electric bus often in the news in the early days, with companies being set up to run fleets of them. But none was really capable of a full day's work economically, and some that were demonstrated never actually ran in service.

The third means of propulsion for motorbuses was

Top:
First results of the LGOC's efforts to build a more reliable vehicle were the 60 'X'-types. They were followed by the famous 'B'-type, the first standardised bus to be built anywhere. *Author's Collection*

Above:
Operator Thomas Tilling was also unhappy with existing commercially-available designs, and wanted a vehicle that was easier to drive. The result was the Tilling TTA1 petrol-electric. *Ian Allan Library*

Left:
AEC and the LGOC were quick to introduce a new design after the end of World War 1. Their 'K'-type of 1919 placed the driver alongside the engine, thus creating room for more passengers. The vehicle also achieved a record low weight per passenger, which has never been bettered. *Author's Collection*

Below left:
Ex-War Department chassis, or chassis built to a similar specification, were bought by numerous operators. This RAF-type Leyland went into service in 1922 with Barnsley & District, the forerunner of Yorkshire Traction. Its Strachan & Brown body had a roller top roof, which could be opened in favourable weather, as shown. *Author's Collection*

Below:
Improvements in the pneumatic tyre offered not only a better ride and less skidding, but also the ability to cover greater distances. They helped particularly the development of the double-decker. Tyre makers worked hard to improve their products and show them to operators. This 22-seat Daimler charabanc was used on demonstrations in 1920, solid tyres often being substituted part way through to underline the improvement brought about by the pneumatic tyres. *Author's Collection*

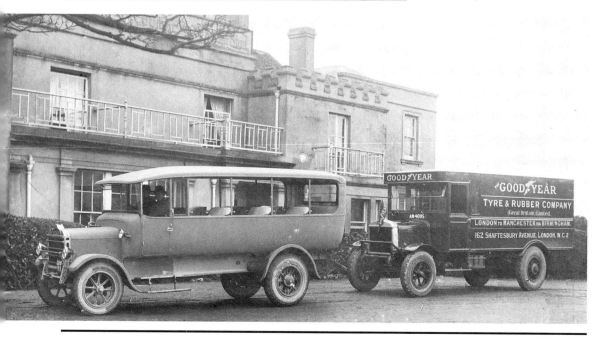

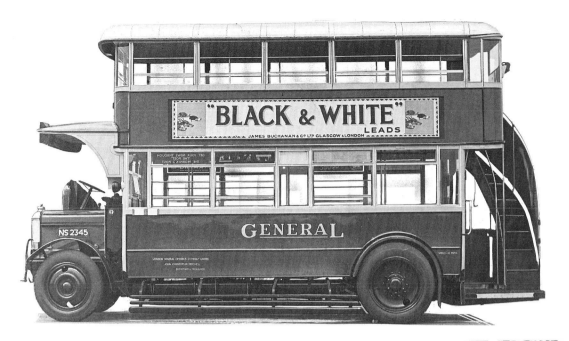

Above:
London General's 'NS' of 1923 was designed with a low chassis frame to take a covered-top body, but it took four years to gain permission to run a fleet in this form. *Author's Collection*

Right:
The chassis of an 'NS' rescued for preservation (and still on solid tyres) shows the dramatic curve of the chassis frame and the angled engine. *Author's Collection*

steam, though that too was to prove a blind alley. The very first Leyland bus was probably a steam-driven single-decker supplied to the Dundee Motor Omnibus Co in 1900, and Thornycroft put a steam double-decker on to a Hammersmith-Oxford Circus service of the London Road Car Co in March 1902. It had steel tyres, a converted horsebus body and a canopy above the upper deck, no doubt to keep the soot and sparks off passengers' heads. But it ran for only two months. The Thornycroft was coal or coke-fired, whereas most subsequent steam buses ran on paraffin. Several makers produced steam buses in the earliest days but there were only two types built in quantity that were of significance: Clarkson and Darracq-Serpollet. Metropolitan Steam Bus began operating in London during 1907, and by 1911 it had more than 50 of the latter double-deckers running. However, before the end of 1912 it had come to an agreement with the LGOC and replaced them all with 'B'-type buses. Its action was prompted no doubt by the bankruptcy of the French maker. A few of the buses and some others

of that make, plus a York-built Gardner-Serpollet, all worked for some years, probably until the mid-1920s, on the Isle of Wight for Ryde, Seaview & District Motor Services. But the best-known steamers were those of Thomas Clarkson. Unable to sell many, he decided to operate them himself, forming the National Steam Car Co in 1909. He built up a fleet of 173 double-deckers on London work; the last was withdrawn in 1919 and a smaller operation of his in Chelmsford did not last much longer.

World War 1 helped develop reliable and durable vehicles, and it also trained thousands of men to drive and repair vehicles. In its aftermath, there was a huge surplus of chassis, in varying states of repair, available cheaply. Enlightened manufacturers such as

Leyland bought as many of their own make as they could and reconditioned them, so that the company's reputation should not suffer.

Many of the vehicles were bodied as buses or charabancs, and were often bought by ex-servicemen who used their war gratuities to help set themselves up in business. Towns such as Harrogate, which at the end of the war were served by two operators, within a few years found themselves with newcomers as well — six in the case of Harrogate.

One big step in bus design was the LGOC's 'K'-type double-decker, first produced in 1919. It put the driver alongside the engine, instead of behind it. This involved changes to the engine, moving all its auxiliaries to the nearside so as to leave enough space for the driver on the offside. Rather more weight was placed on the front axle, but the bus seated 46, instead of the 34 of older designs. Part of the gain in capacity came from a modest relaxation of the width limit, which permitted forward-facing seats instead of all inward-facing ones on the lower deck. This forward-control layout, as it came to be called, eventually became standard on heavy-duty bus chassis, although not all makers followed quickly. The 'K'-type was also noteworthy in having the lowest unladen weight per passenger of any bus. A further development in London was the 'S'-type, with 54 seats in double-deck form; it needed a relaxation in the weight regulations before it became legal.

More significant was the LGOC's 'NS'-type, built of course by AEC. The company was anxious to fit covered tops to its double-deckers, since in inclement weather many would not use the upper deck. Most electric trams had had roofs for some years. So the chassis of the 'NS' was not straight-framed, with springs and axles simply hung below, but curved steeply downwards immediately behind the engine and front wheels, arched itself over the rear axle and finally lowered itself even closer to the ground to give a step height of little more than 12in (300mm). More important was the lowered centre of gravity, which the company hoped would make the covered top

acceptable to the Metropolitan Police. Eventually it did, but not before over 1,700 open-top 'NSs' had entered service. Approval for covered-top 'NSs' came in 1926. Ironically, Birmingham Corporation had gained approval for covered-top bodies in 1924 on high-frame AEC 504 chassis — the provincial version of the 'S'-type.

The achievement of the 'NS' was not merely in designing a satisfactory low chassis frame; mechanical components had to be altered or improved as well. For example, the relatively primitive lubrication system of the engine had to be made to cope with its angled mounting, which was necessary to line it up with the rear axle. For the first time, a bus chassis was significantly different from that of a goods vehicle.

For operators and manufacturers the most significant development in the 1920s was the pneumatic tyre, which gradually became a practical (and economic) proposition on larger buses and coaches. Increasing use of pneumatics coincided with a big surge in imported chassis, mainly from the USA. Its enormous domestic market offered economies of scale which permitted sales to the UK at low prices. Chassis often had six-cylinder engines and gave buses and coaches which could often out-perform established UK makes. But US supplies were ultimately strangled by imposition of import duties in the late 1920s and these in turn led to the establishment of the Bedford marque in the UK.

The coach market developed substantially in the
1920s, and became highly competitive. Small operators' purchasing decisions were often made on the
cheapness of the hire purchase payments offered,
rather than the durability of the vehicle.

Six-wheelers enjoyed an initial success in the mid
to late 1920s, mainly because of doubts over the reliability of pneumatic tyres; Guy and Karrier did particularly well in this field. However, as tyres improved,
the added complexity and weight went against the
layout, and in the early to mid-1930s only operators
who wanted relatively high capacity vehicles bought
them; six-wheelers offered an extra few feet in length.

If there was a single event that changed the face of
the bus industry it was the introduction of the Leyland
Titan double-decker. This was designed by
G. J. Rackham and was unveiled in 1927. Its low
frame height, use of pneumatic tyres of reasonable
size, coupled with a patented upper-deck layout with
dropped gangway, gave a low overall height that
allowed widespread use of double-deckers outside
towns and cities for the first time. In themselves most
features of the Titan, such as the six-cylinder engines
or four-wheel brakes, were not new, but the total
combination was. This was one reason for the Titan's
success, while Gilford's more revolutionary double-
decker a few years later was an utter failure. The
Titan was just one of a family of double and single-
deck models whose main attributes were to be copied

by virtually every successful chassis builder in the
1930s.

New legislation was shortly to make its mark on
the industry. Construction & Use Regulations laid
down lengths, widths, gangway widths, seat spacing,
tilt tests and also ended the more extreme rebuilds of
vehicles such as those practised by the Barton
Brothers. A licensing system for routes and timings
introduced at the same time gave established operators protection. Together these measures killed off
most of the remaining imports of small chassis, and
several UK makers as well. But the licensing system,
despite some unfairness, provided security for operators and that allowed them to make large-scale invest-
ments in new vehicles. The bus industry became one
of relative prosperity at a time when the country as a
whole was still depressed. The availability of quali-
fied and skilled engineers at relatively low salaries
launched the bus industry on a path of rapid improvement. Oil (or diesel) engines came in during the early
1930s. Early models were often found wanting, but
within a few years they had been developed as
successful and reliable, and were far more economical
to run than petrol engines.

These modern, durable designs permitted large-
scale replacement of many tram systems. 'Buy a Titan
and bury a tram' said the famous Leyland advert. For
political, economic and other reasons many trams
were little changed from their form in the early 1900s,
and Titans, AEC Regents and Daimler double-deckers
were well able to replace them. Such sales again
improved the total volume from these makers and this
not only added to the economies of scale they enjoyed
but also allowed further funds to be used for more
research and development, which again put them
ahead of smaller makers such as Thornycroft.

From the early 1930s there were trials with alternative engine positions. Of these, the AEC 'Q'-type

achieved the highest volume of sales (which, even so, totalled just 348 chassis), and Leyland and the London Passenger Transport Board later in the decade developed the underfloor-engined single-decker (of which 88 were built). Midland Red produced four prototypes with rear engines, subsequently rebuilding them to an underfloor-engined layout; and AEC produced an underfloor-engined prototype for Canada in 1939.

Leyland also tried the rear engine position and, after trials with one prototype, went on to build 48 smaller single-deckers of this type for the LPTB. Maudslay had reasonable success with a set-back front axle design which still retained a vertical engine at the front, but provided room for up to 40 seats.

The outbreak of World War 2 first slowed and then halted PSV production. Subsequently makers were allowed to complete building vehicles on which work had already begun; these were known as 'unfrozen'

vehicles. New production was resumed under Government control and utility vehicles were produced. Single-deckers came solely from Bedford (the OWB, which was petrol-engined) and double-deckers initially from Guy (a surprising choice) and subsequently from Daimler and Bristol as well. Designs were basic with no use of chrome, aluminium or other materials in short supply. The same restrictions and others as well were applied to bodybuilders, with opening windows being limited to one per side per deck and, later, wooden slatted seats only being permitted. Strangely, the same restrictions did not always apply to vehicles that were rebodied, and at least one bodybuilder was allowed to go on using its standard metal frame body design. However, very poor timber framing was the worst feature of most utility bodies, and that was something beyond the control of the bodybuilders.

Three factors brought about the need for unfrozen

Above:
G. J. Rackham took a poor view of six-wheelers, considering them unnecessary, dated and unlikely to sell in quantity. However, mainly because of LGOC's enthusiasm for the type, AEC was to supply the operator with well over 1,400 chassis in just three years. This is the prototype double-deck AEC Renown when new. *Author's Collection*

Right:
Guy and Karrier had been pioneers of six-wheelers. Great claims were made for the advantages of six-wheel vehicles, and in the early days of giant pneumatic tyres, they might have had some merit. In front of Karrier's first of the type is posed comedian Wee Georgie Wood (far right) and others of a similar build. *Geoff Lumb Collection*

and utility vehicles. Older vehicles were continuing to wear out, some operators had vehicles destroyed in air raids, and the number of passengers carried had increased enormously as factories turned to war production and more factories — often in rural areas inaccessible by any other means — were specially built. However, wartime allocation of new vehicles (and indeed, spare parts as well) was under a Government bureaucracy, with its own interpretation of need. Particularly in its early days, this bureaucracy seemed quite unable to take account of operators' existing fleet composition. Operator A, with Leylands, might get two AECs, while operator B, with mainly AECs, would get three Leylands — all unfrozen examples, of course. Even worse was allocation of bodybuilder, with seven identical chassis for one operator, for example, carrying three different makes of body.

Another example of wartime stringency was Government plans for most operators to use 'producer gas' fuel for a proportion of their fleets. Petrol-engined vehicles were more suited for this conversion, which generally involved towing a two-wheel trailer. Coke or anthracite was burnt in the trailer to produce the gas. Considerable numbers of these trailers were manufactured, but operators were, not surprisingly, reluctant to use them. Those who did found power output was very low, so hilly routes were out of the question. Engine life was also reduced. London found it had to move stops to the far side of bridges over railways, as restarting on a rising gradient with a full load could prove impossible. Luckily, fuel supplies began to improve — all liquid fuel was imported in those days — and many trailers were scrapped without being used.

In the later part of the war some manufacturers and bodybuilders were permitted to develop and build prototypes of planned postwar designs. Later the austerity specification was modified; upholstered seats, more opening windows, polished aluminium radiator shells and other features all returned.

Wartime buses may not have appeared particularly attractive, but they were reliable and ran high mileages with the minimum of attention. Many utilities, and indeed many 1930s vehicles, often rebodied, survived in active service into the middle and late 1950s, while some lasted into the early 1960s. In 45 years the British bus industry had come a long way.

Above:
Replacement of worn-out tram systems by buses boosted business for AEC, Leyland and Daimler in the 1930s. Leyland had a slogan 'buy a Titan and bury a tram' — this Titan TD1 was doing just that at Bradford, though here trolleybuses later also replaced many trams. *Author's Collection*

Left:
Modern buses were bound to be more attractive to the public than ageing tramcars, which often ran on worn-out track. The Tynemouth & District Traction Co replaced trams on its North Shields-Whitley Bay coastal route with these AECs in 1931, but 'via tram route' continued to be part of the destination displays for many years. *Ian Allan Library*

Left:
The new breed of relatively lively, low buses meant the end of older vehicles, though many World War 1 designs had lasted well. This former War Department Daimler 'Y'-type of Potteries had had its wheelbase extended, and was not withdrawn until 1930. *Ian Allan Library*

Below:
Makers lost no opportunity to promote their products. To coincide with the announcement of the Regent in October 1929, AEC's first prototype made a 12hr non-stop 500-mile continuous run round the Brooklands race track. It averaged 41mph and speeds were said to have reached 50mph at times. AEC went on to deliver over 1,000 chassis in the first year of production. *Author's Collection*

Left:
AEC was the first UK commercial vehicle maker to install a moving track on which chassis were built. But another much smaller company to track build was Gilford, pictured here. Its models enjoyed enormous success, mainly with smaller operators, but later these sold out to larger companies (or just faded away) and a subsequent obsession in developing a revolutionary low-floor double-decker (which proved unsaleable) ultimately killed the company. *Author's Collection*

Above:
AEC did not rest on its laurels. Late in 1932 a prototype side-engined bus with single wheels all round and virtually all floorspace given over to passenger accommodation appeared on the streets of London. It was the first of the 'Q'-type. *Author's Collection*

Right:
Double-deck variants of the 'Q' were also built. They offered an unrivalled front-entrance layout that would have been ideal for one-man operation, except that there was no requirement for it; 20 or (later) 26 seats were the most permitted on a one-man operated bus for many years. *Ian Allan Library*

Below:
A major development in the early 1930s was that of the oil (or diesel, or compression ignition) engine. Here at AEC's special Oil Engine Show at Southall in November 1930 are members of the Municipal Tramways & Transport Association. Among the vehicles they are inspecting is (left) one of the first three Regents (the LGOC 'ST'-type) to be fitted with the AEC-Acro 8.1 litre oil engine, the first to be offered commercially. However, it was not until AEC called in Ricardo to help with a redesign that the engine became reliable. *Author's Collection*

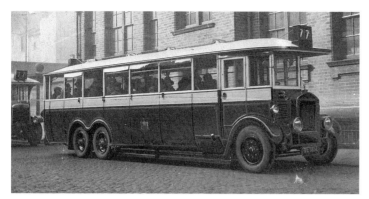

Left:
Mercedes-Benz was an undoubted pioneer of the oil engine and Sheffield Corporation put this Karrier six-wheeler into service in 1930 with a Mercedes diesel under the bonnet. It was probably much more reliable (and more economical) than it had ever been with a Karrier engine. *Author's Collection*

Above:
A surprising move saw Tilling divest itself of Tilling-Stevens, which reformed as TSM. For a few years the new company did well with conventional petrol-engined models, but began to lose out after Tilling bought Bristol. This TSM with Strachan body was a 'one off' purchase by Aldershot & District early in 1932. It had been exhibited at the 1931 motor show in the operator's colours. *Ian Allan Library*

Left:
Daimler built up a considerable business with municipal operators in the 1930s, much of it with the help of the legendary Gardner engine. It still built cars as well. This is the new passenger vehicle bay at the factory, complete with bus chassis, that came into use in 1934. *Ian Allan Library*

Above:
Not all the successes of the 1930s were with heavier diesel-engined chassis. Bedford sold nothing but light, mass produced, petrol-engined chassis in large numbers. The Duple-bodied coach was the most popular version; this is one new to Southern National in 1939. It seated 25. *J. Taylor*

Right:
With Tilling Group backing, Bristol established itself as a major builder in the 1930s, making increasing use of Gardner diesel engines. A mid-1930s JO5G of United Automobile Services is guided through a tight corner in Hawes, North Yorkshire. *Author*

Right:
Interest in alternative engine positions continued, even if AEC's 'Q' had not sold well. L. G. Wyndham Shire, Midland Red's chief engineer, designed and built four rear-engined PSVs in 1935-36. These had petrol engines and entrances ahead of the front axle. Here Wyndham Shire stands by one of the bus versions. *Ian Allan Library*

Right:
Next to move the engine position was Maudslay. This is the 1937 Commercial Motor Show exhibit, the SF40, later renamed the Magna. About 100 were built between 1935 and 1939, with Maudslay petrol or Gardner diesel vertical engines and a set-back front axle that allowed 40 seats. *Author's Collection*

Above:
Tilling-Stevens' Successor of 1937 had a three-axle chassis with independent rear suspension. Its eight-cylinder 7.45 litre diesel engine was a horizontally-opposed unit of flat or underfloor layout, had twin fuel pumps and drove through a seven-speed preselector gearbox. Two chassis were built and one bodied (by Duple, as illustrated) but no operator ever ran one; probably Tilling-Stevens lacked the resources to develop the design. *Author's Collection*

Above:
Less successful was the other LPTB-Leyland, a small rear-engined bus. Teething troubles and the onset of war (when larger, not smaller buses were needed) gave all 49 vehicles a chequered career. They had a vertical engine with the radiator behind it. A bodied example is pictured on page 27. *Author's Collection*

Right:
There could be fewer greater contrasts with Leyland's success than that of Maudslay, struggling along and selling chassis mainly in single figures. Thus Neath & Cardiff Luxury Coaches represented one of the manufacturer's largest customers, buying a total of seven SF40 or Magna chassis. This is one of four with Gardner engine and striking Duple bodywork delivered in 1939. *Author's Collection*

Below:
Some operators preferred rear entrances, others front entrances on single-deckers. But both municipal and company operators in Scotland were the main enthusiasts for this style of 'cut away' rear entrance (with or without door). This SMT AEC Regal dates from 1938. In 1955 it was one of a number to lose their Alexander bodies and receive new Burlingham coach bodies. *Gavin Booth Collection*

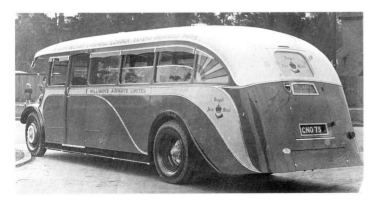

Left:
Many independent operators vanished in the early 1930s, unable to gain licences for what they were already operating. Entrepreneur Edward Hillman began coach operation in east London in 1928 and within three years had over 100 Gilfords in his fleet. Many were compulsorily acquired by the LPTB in 1934, but Hillman had also begun air services. In 1935 the link from central London to his Essex airport was provided by two of these Gilford Heras with Wycombe bodies and reinforced bullion compartments at the rear. *Author's Collection*

Left:
Some coach operators probably bought AEC 'Qs' or Maudslay SF40s for the improved appearance at the front. Bus operators also became keen on projecting a modern image. Leeds Corporation, after buying somewhat dated-looking double-deck bodywork, then took two striking full-fronted double-deckers on AEC Regent chassis. One was fitted with MCW bodywork and the other with Roe. Subsequently a new Roe body for Leeds of distinctive appearance became a regular motor show tradition. *Ian Allan Library*

Left:
London's RT type chassis of 1938 represented the peak of development of the conventional front-engined bus. Use of such a large engine — 9.6 litres — in the interest of long life and economy was new. Air brakes had been tried before (on trolleybuses) but the air-operated pre-selector gearbox was new. Flexible engine mountings, high driving position, automatic brake adjustment and chassis lubrication combined with other features to produce a design that was still ahead of its time 15 years later. Just one chassis, pictured, went outside London — to Glasgow in 1940. Its Weymann body was similar to others supplied to Glasgow. *Ian Allan Library*

Right:
Having first built one rear-engined prototype for evaluation, with a transverse petrol engine, Leyland went on in conjunction with London Transport to develop a 20-seat rear-engined version of the Cub. One prototype and 59 production versions were planned. The vertical diesel engine was mounted in line with the chassis, and gearbox and worm-driven rear axle were mounted as one unit. War intervened and only 49 were built. War also reduced the need for small buses and teething troubles were never properly solved. *Author's Collection*

Left:
Just ahead of the rear-engined Leyland came development of a full-sized underfloor-engined single-decker, again in conjunction with LT. A horizontal version of Leyland's 8.6 litre diesel engine was mounted on the offside of the chassis below floor level immediately behind the driver. Some 87 production versions followed for LT as sightseeing or Green Line coaches. The driving position on the prototype was very high (it seems to have been an LT obsession at the time) and this picture shows angles of vision being checked on the incomplete vehicle at Leyland. *Author's Collection*

Right:
The onset of war soon cut short the supply of new vehicles and many operators also lost existing vehicles requisitioned for military use. This elderly Maudslay was used as a mobile gunnery school for Merchant Navy personnel. Pupils are learning to aim at a model aircraft running on wires suspended from the outside of the bus. *Ian Allan Library*

Right:
Only one utility single-deck type was made, the Bedford OWB. Three bodybuilders — Duple (which did the design), Roe and Scottish Motor Traction — constructed the bodies to an identical specification. Many large operators took none, perhaps because they did not want petrol engines, but others took a quantity. Two Belfast Corporation examples await workers from the shipyards. *Author's Collection*

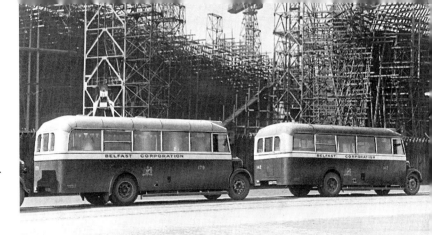

Right:
Many vehicles were rebodied to replace worn-out or war-damaged bodywork. But the Scottish Bus Group replaced many single-deck bodies with new double-deck ones. This Western SMT 1937 Leyland Tiger originally had an Alexander coach body, but it, along with 45 others, was rebuilt to Titan specification and fitted with a new lowbridge utility Alexander double-deck body. *Author*

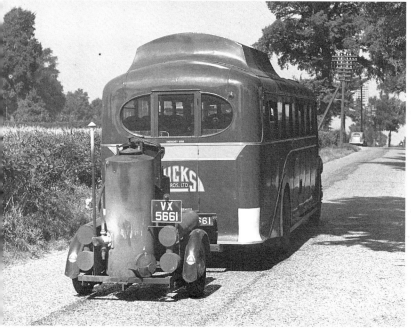

Above:
In World War 1 some operators voluntarily used town gas to overcome fuel shortages. Chapman & Sons of Eastbourne — a famous pioneering operator which ultimately sold out to Southdown — fitted this Dennis charabanc with wooden tray and inflatable bag. The equipment was probably provided by Barton Brothers, which developed similar equipment for its own fleet. *Author's Collection*

Left:
World War 2 ultimately saw the Government leaning heavily on operators to use anthracite-burning producer gas trailers to power a proportion of their fleet, and thus save scarce imported fuel. This 1940 picture shows a prototype installation developed by Eastern National and towed by a Leyland of Hicks Bros of Braintree. Each trailer used about one ton of home-produced anthracite a week. *Author's Collection*

Right:
During the war manufacturers were allowed to produce the occasional prototype of what they hoped to build when the war was over. Midland Red substantially reworked its four experimental rear-engined single-deckers; they reappeared with an underfloor-engined layout that became standard when the company resumed building its own buses. *Birmingham & Midland Museum of Transport Collection*

Above:
After the war shortages remained and operators had to cope with even greater numbers of passengers with elderly fleets. Prominent in this early postwar view at Oxford are a veteran Maudslay double-decker of Charlton on Otmoor Services and a United Counties Bristol JO5G-ECW coach of 1937. *W. T. Lambden*

Right:
Many operators solved part of their problems by having prewar chassis rebodied. Because of the poor quality of the materials used, many wartime bodies soon also needed rebuilding if not replacement. This Bristol Tramways double-decker is not a Bristol, despite its radiator, but a rebuilt wartime Guy now carrying an older body built by the operator. *Ian Allan Library*

ADC

Daimler had had a close relationship with AEC before World War 1, and this was followed by the creation of a joint company, Associated Daimler Co, in 1926, to share components but with most chassis being built at AEC, first at Walthamstow and then at its new Southall factory.

The relationship lasted only to 1928, after which the partners went their separate ways. Not all the models built under the ADC banner were new. In 1927 there was the 'LS' or London Six, a cumbersome six-wheeler (mainly a double-decker) of which most went to London General and were fitted with Daimler's six-cylinder sleeve-valve engine. More modern were a pair of forward and normal control models of modest weight, the 423 and 424, some of which had the Daimler engine. Surprisingly, they were built at Coventry, and carried no name or initials on their radiators. The most successful was the earlier forward-control 416, which had a frame almost as low as the 'NS', a new gearbox and a choice of AEC or Daimler engine. Nearly, 1,000 were sold in two-and-a-half years.

Left:
The most successful ADC chassis was the 416, available with AEC's four-cylinder 5.1 litre engine or Daimler's six-cylinder, sleeve-valve engine of just 3.5 litres. This 1927 example with Massey body went to the Isle of Man and later joined the fleet of Isle of Man Road Services. *Author's Collection*

Centre left:
Greenock & Port Glasgow Tramways had bought a batch of 'NS'-type ADC double-deckers in 1925-26, and in 1928 tried this ADC 802 for two months. None were, however, bought. The model had been hastily designed to meet competition from the new Guy and Karrier six-wheelers, but won virtually no orders. Two became AEC staff buses, one having 104 seats. They ferried staff between Walthamstow and the new AEC factory at Southall. *Ian Allan Library*

Bottom left:
This ADC 423 with United Auto body was a new chassis, built by Daimler at Coventry and fitted with Daimler's sleeve-valve, six-cylinder engine. Built for exhibition at the 1927 Commercial Motor Show, the bus was subsequently bought by Crosville to become only one of two non-Leyland full-size buses in the fleet. It is pictured at AEC's Southall works before delivery. *Ian Allan Library*

Left:
An example of AEC's 3-4-ton chassis, as built between
1915 and 1919 and here fitted with a charabanc body.
This one is unusual in having a central gangway. Note
the double running board. This vehicle had a Tylor
engine. *Author's Collection*

AEC

Most manufacturers begin in a small way, but the
Associated Equipment Co was a separation from the
vehicle building works of the London General
Omnibus Co at Walthamstow and, therefore, started
in June 1912 with large-scale production already
under way. It was a subsidiary of the London
Underground Group (like the LGOC) and no doubt
the separation was intended to facilitate sales to other
operators, but the full order book meant that there
were none for over a year. The first major customer
was United Automobile, but the outside sales were
made by Daimler, with which an agreement had
meanwhile been concluded. These vehicles carried
Daimler on the radiator, and many had Daimler
engines.

Later, in 1926, there was another joint arrangement
with Daimler: chassis were built (first at
Walthamstow and then at AEC's new factory at
Southall) as Associated Daimlers and fitted with
engines by either maker. This arrangement broke up
in 1928 at about the same time as the legendary
G. J. Rackham was poached from Leyland — he said
he couldn't stand the Lancashire weather — as chief
engineer of AEC.

During World War 1 AEC had built some 8,000
'Y'-type chassis for the War Department. It was a
heavier version of the 'B', with larger engine,
conventional gearbox and pressed steel chassis frame
(that of the 'B'-type was flitched timber). Production
for civilian use continued after the war, some having
Daimler sleeve-valve engines. Many were bodied as
buses. New models were the 'K'-type of 1919, in
which the driver was moved alongside the engine, and
the later, larger 'S'-type (which still retained a
flitched timber chassis). Vehicles for other than the
LGOC were later known by type numbers: 301 for the
'K'; 401 for the 'S'; and, 501 for improved 'Y'-types.

A huge step forward came with the 'NS', which
had a drop frame of steel, designed to lower the centre
of gravity of the vehicle, and — hopefully —
persuade the Metropolitan Police to allow the upper
deck to be roofed. Technically it was a remarkable
achievement in aligning the propshafts of an engine
high above the front axle with a chassis-mounted
gearbox and a low rear axle with underslung worm
drive.

Major leaps in design came with G. J. Rackham,
the first being a new six-cylinder overhead camshaft
engine. Owing more than a passing resemblance to
that which he had designed for Leyland, it went into
production within months. It was fitted into the
416/426 chassis, now the Reliance model 660. It
transformed the vehicle and enabled AEC to more
than use up the stocks of chassis parts it already had.
It sold to many coach operators who liked its smooth
and quite powerful engine.

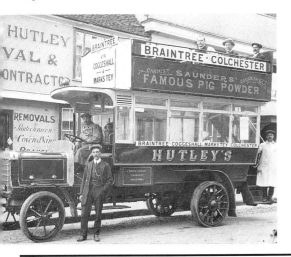

Left:
This is a very standard 'B'-type chassis of 1914, albeit
operated by Arthur Hutley of Braintree, Essex. He had
bought the bus from the Daimler Co of Pall Mall,
London — at the start of the co-operation between the
two makers. *Author's Collection*

The next step was the Regal single- and Regent double-deckers, announced in 1929. With nicely curved dropframes, these had a more compact front end than their Leyland equivalents, and the new engine. There was also a six-wheeled version, the Renown, which was disliked by Rackham but taken up enthusiastically by the LGOC to make it by far the best-selling six-wheeler on the market.

AEC was early into developing oil engines (as diesels were then usually called) and, after the usual teething problems, developed a reliable 8.8 litre engine in 1931, soon adding a 7.7 litre unit as well. Both benefited from Ricardo combustion chamber design. From 1932 AECs were offered with fluid transmission, which greatly eased urban bus driving. London standardised on it. Initially, Daimler, which had developed the fluid coupling and Wilson-type epicyclic gearbox, supplied complete units to AEC.

The creation of the London Passenger Transport Board in July 1933 to take over all local bus and coach (along with tram and trolleybus) operations in the London area brought about the total separation of AEC, though the LPTB continued to buy most of its buses and coaches from the company.

There were two other notable developments. The first was the 'Q'-type, with engine mounted behind the offside front wheel. Designed by Rackham chiefly as a double-decker, it sold mainly as a single-decker; a total of 348 chassis were built, of which only 23 were double-deckers. With an entrance ahead of the (set back) front axle, the staircase could rise neatly over the engine and front wheel. The design deserved to do better; 20 years later most of its features could be found on new underfloor-engined single-deckers.

The other development was production, from 1939, of 150 of London's 'RT'-type to meet a new specification. With larger engine (9.6 litres) and air brakes, its features too were later to be widely copied.

Above:
United Automobile was a big buyer of AECs after World War 1. These six buses with 45hp chassis were part of a 1919 order for 50. The four on the right have rudimentary double-deck bodywork of a rather basic style used by the company at the time. The chassis was the same for either.
Author's Collection

Right:
Better remembered for its coaches, Greyhound was also a bus operator. This 'NS' supplied in 1925 was similar to those running in London, though later Greyhound had pneumatic-tyred examples. Note the man perched alongside the driver. Greyhound was later taken over by Bristol Tramways. *Author's Collection*

Top:
This AEC Reliance was one of the first to be fitted with the new Rackham-designed six-cylinder engine that transformed the model. It entered service with East Surrey Traction in November 1928; the new model 660 Reliance was not announced until January 1929. The bus had a Hall Lewis 32-seat dual-door body, and is seen outside the old (now demolished) Reigate garage.
Ian Allan Library

Above:
Dundee Corporation operated this AEC Regent double-decker with oil engine and Park Royal 50-seat bus body from July 1932 until 1949. Originally a demonstrator, it was bought from AEC in October 1932, and was among the first diesel-engined vehicles in the fleet.
Rex Kennedy Collection

Left:
Despite Rackham's misgivings about the concept, AEC's six-wheeled Renown sold in numbers for a few years, and there were isolated further sales in the late 1930s. The LGOC was the biggest customer, buying some 1,400. Though most were double-deckers, there were 200 single-deckers, some of which were to prove the longest-lived. Nearly half of them gained AEC 7.7 litre diesel engines from scrapped (and newer) London STLs, and some had bodywork substantially rebuilt (as here) to enable them to survive until 1952. *Tony Bunce*

Centre left:
The biggest fleet of AEC Regents was bought by London Transport. Some 2,000 of the style illustrated, with 56-seat body, AEC 7.7 litre diesel engine, fluid flywheel and pre-selector gearbox, were bought up to 1939, with the last surviving in London until 1954. This one is seen, in 1955, working for Premier Travel of Cambridge. *Author*

Below:
A production example of AEC and LT's joint design, the RT, is seen at Victoria in postwar years. The war stopped production at 150 vehicles, delivered between October 1939 and January 1942. Shortages of materials because of the war effort delayed body production in particular. *Author*

AJS

Better known for its motorcycles, A. J. Stevens & Co (1914) of Wolverhampton built PSVs for just three years — 1929-31 — at a time when sales of motorcycles were poor. There were three models, all with Coventry Climax petrol engines: the Pilot, designed as a 26-seater in either normal or forward-control layout; the forward-control 32-seat Commodore; and — finally — the Admiral which was introduced in 1931 and, therefore, had a very short production run. In October 1931 the company went into liquidation. Design of the Pilot is said to have been based on the Star Flyer, designs for which were passed on by Guy after it bought Star. All three makes were built in the same town.

Below:
A forward-control AJS Commodore is put through its paces over the *Modern Transport* test route on a wet 1930 day. A year later the company had gone. The Commodore had a Coventry Climax petrol engine. *Ian Allan Library*

Bottom:
A normal-control version of the AJS Pilot fitted with luxury coach body complete with two hinged doors. It was supplied to the Central Garage of Longford, Coventry. *Ian Allan Library*

Albion

Like many others, the Albion Motor Car Co began by making cars and dogcarts. However, it decided to give up cars in 1912 when it found that over two-thirds of total production was of commercial vehicles. Despite this it took until 1931 for the company name to be changed to Albion Motors. Over the years the company earned a reputation for solid, no-frills engineering exemplified perhaps by the way it still offered four-cylinder engines as an option when most others had ceased to build them. For all that, it survived the depression years when rivals such as Halley folded.

Albion began in 1899, upstairs, in 3,600sq ft of space above the Clan Line repair shops in Glasgow. It was started by Norman O. Fulton and T. Blackwood Murray, who had previously been, respectively, works manager and commercial manager at car maker Arrol-Johnston. The first vehicle was produced in 1900. By 1902 Albion was offering half-ton vans and, by 1903, had moved to much larger premises at Scotstoun, Glasgow. Larger vans soon followed and 1910 saw the introduction of the A10, a 32hp model with monobloc four-cylinder engine, chain drive and a patent engine governor and lubricator. Before World War 1 the company had built up an impressive clientele for PSVs, including Wolverhampton Corporation Tramways, David MacBrayne and the Largs, Wemyss Bay & West Coast Motor Service of Largs. Some 6,000 A10 lorries were supplied to the War Department between 1914 and 1918, and production continued into the 1920s.

New models included a 20hp 1½-tonner, while 1923 saw the introduction of the Viking for up to 18 seats, with a relatively low frame height; just one step was needed, it was said. A drop-frame range, the 26 Series, was introduced in October 1925, not that long after AEC's pioneering 'NS'. As with the earlier 24

Series a variety of wheelbases was offered. The first forward-control chassis came in 1927. It was called the Viking PM28 and used the same 30/60hp engine as the 26 Series. Scottish Motor Traction placed one order for 24 PM28s in March 1927, and by the end of 1929 had become a big Albion user, with nearly 90 of various types bought from 1926 onwards. By 1930 there were forward and normal-control Vikings, with four and six-cylinder engines, the last-named being called Viking Sixes. Vikings were phased out in 1931-32.

The Valkyrie came in at the end of 1930 with a 60bhp five-litre four-cylinder engine. It was replaced from 1933 with a 6.1 litre four-cylinder engine; by this time diesels were an option. Albion had not been particularly quick to develop its own diesels, and had, therefore, offered Beardmore, Dorman and Gardner units. These continued to be fitted after Albion had designed its own diesel. New Valkyrie models came again in 1935, with one offering a 110bhp 7.8 litre six-cylinder unit. The same petrol engine was also available in the Valiant, and soon this powerful version of the Valkyrie replaced it. Valiants were less popular, lasting from 1931 to 1936, and were forward-control chassis bigger than the Viking Six and more powerful than the Valkyrie. Yet another model running at the same time was the Victor. First designed as a 20-seater, of normal-control layout with a 42bhp 3.15 litre engine, it soon gained a 60bhp 3.62

Below:
Despite its early concentration on commercials, it took Albion a long time to change its name, as the background to the picture shows. The chassis is a normal-control, low-frame model. The relatively neat front end contrasts with that achieved on forward-control versions at the same time. *Ian Allan Library*

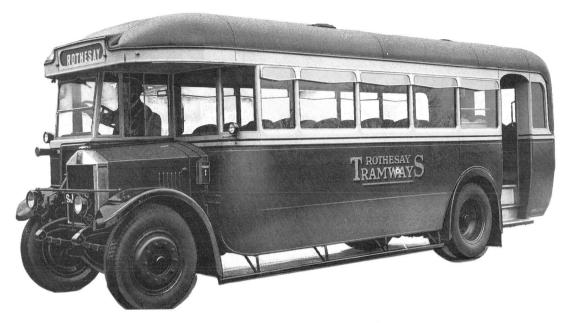

Above:
Rothesay Tramways took delivery of a batch of these Albion 30/60hp models in 1930. The 32-seat bodies featured an angled front bulkhead window on the nearside. The operator was later owned by Western SMT and still later merged into it. *Author's Collection*

Right:
No doubt the sight of all those AEC and Leyland double-deckers in service in Glasgow spurred Albion to offer a double-deck chassis. All told, Glasgow Corporation bought 130 in the years up to 1939, though Albion did not always gain a share of the annual orders. Fifteen of these Venturers, with Albion's own new 9.08 litre diesel engine and Cowieson 56-seat all-metal bodies, were delivered in 1938, alongside 85 AEC Regents. *Author's Collection*

Right:
Red & White Services was a strong Albion supporter in the 1930s, and also ran a couple of dealerships for the make. This CX11, with centre-entrance Duple body, dates from 1939. It is pictured (despite the fleetname) working for Bristol Tramways in Stroud in 1953 after an exchange of territory and vehicles with Red & White. A further exchange of territory the following year saw the bus returned to Red & White. *M. J. Mogridge*

litre unit. Further changes included forward-control models and a 65bhp 3.89 litre engine. Most were sold as coach chassis. The model lasted up to 1939 by which time 30 seats were the norm.

Albion's first venture into double-deckers came late in 1932 with the Venturer. Initially this was fitted with a 6.85 litre petrol engine or a Gardner diesel and had a seating capacity of up to 51. The 1935 Venturer could have up to 55 seats, and a larger 7.8 litre petrol engine developing 103bhp was an option as was a Gardner. The 1937 Commercial Motor Show saw the launch of the first of the CX series of models, which at last had the engine and gearbox mounted in one unit, a feature previously found only on the light Victor. Valkyrie CXs could have 6.1 litre four-cylinder or 9.1 litre six-cylinder petrol engines, Albion's own diesel, or Gardner 5LW or 6LW diesels fitted; some even had Gardner 4LWs. Venturer CXs had just Albion's 9.1 litre diesel as standard and Gardner 6LW or Albion petrol engines as options.

There was also, for a time, a high-capacity six-wheel single-decker. It was a version of the Valkyrie, with Young's Bus Service of Paisley (later to become part of Western SMT) buying 15 in 1937-38. They had cumbersome-looking Cowieson bus bodies seating 39.

All-British or ABC

George Johnston, formerly the Johnston in Arrol-Johnston, formed the All-British Car Co of Glasgow in 1906. It built and ran its own bus or buses — perhaps as many as six — in London for just a few months in 1907. They were of remarkably squat design, said to be 1ft 4in (400mm) lower than other open-top double-deckers, helped by the sunken gangway on the lower deck. A horizontal four-cylinder engine was mounted compactly over the front wheels. The chassis was said to be guaranteed for three years, and the company had an agreement (spectacularly unfulfilled) to sell 250 buses through a

sister company, the London-based All-British Chassis Bus Co.

In 1908 three ABC double-deckers went into service with Autocar of Tunbridge Wells, and one of them was still used as a spare bus in 1914.

Alldays

Alldays & Onions Pneumatic Engineering Co of Birmingham could trace its ancestry back to 1650. Some 253 years later it started building cars, followed by vans and then, in 1911, trucks with a 40hp engine. In that same year it also built the chassis for the first Railless trolleybuses. Though it never offered motorbus chassis as such, Sir William Lever (of Lever Brothers and Port Sunlight fame) began a bus service with one (plus one Star) in June 1914.

However, in World War 1, West Bridgford UDC, situated on the outskirts of Nottingham, bought a total of seven Alldays chassis. Five replaced virtually new Dennis bus chassis which had been taken over by the War Office. The Alldays were chain driven, which the War Office did not favour. Each chassis cost £595, and the first five took the registrations of the earlier Dennis quintet (a habit not uncommon in those days) as well as the latter's Dodson 32-seat double-deck bodies. The last remaining Alldays were sold by West Bridgford in 1921, one or two seeing subsequent service with another operator.

Argus

Argus was one of Germany's smaller makes and was in business for about four years. The Manx Electric Railway, on the Isle of Man, ran two of the type with charabanc bodies from 1907 until the outbreak of World War 1. The duo operated a summer service from a station on Snaefell Mountain Railway to a nearby beauty spot.

Argyll

Cars and then vans based on car chassis were the early products of this Glasgow-based company, which traded from 1902 until 1914. By 1904 there was a 15cwt (^{3}/4 ton) model, and within a couple of years an even bigger range was available; taxis and fire appliances were subsequently added.

Left:
In terms of design this Argyll bus was a sturdy-looking product from what had been previously just a car maker. Rows of seats are raised towards the rear to improve visibility for passengers, though the mail compartment behind the driver did not permit much forward visibility for them. *Author's Collection*

Left:
This Armstrong-Whitworth, owned by Vanguard, is seen in 1908, just after it entered service with the London operator. *Author's Collection*

Arrol-Johnston

This Scottish maker began with cars and then offered a charabanc on a lengthened car chassis. Proper commercial vehicle and passenger chassis were announced in 1905 and were later followed by another PSV chassis with the driver seated alongside the engine. This had a 5.1 litre four-cylinder unit with detachable heads, whereas previous vehicles had had three-cylinder engines. Though some space was saved on the new model, the driver was positioned rather to the back of the engine, with a heavily-raked steering column reaching back to him. The model was successful in that a batch of 30 were sold to the Great Eastern Railway and fitted with conventional open-top double-deck bodies.

Not so successful were two earlier charabancs bought by the North British Railway in 1905; they broke down so often that for 1906 the summer-only service they ran was reduced so that one was spare while the other worked. Problems continued and in 1907 Arrol-Johnston undertook some kind of part exchange deal. The company took the vehicles back and refitted the bodywork to two new chassis, which proved more reliable.

The last Arrol-Johnstons were made in 1915.

Armstrong-Whitworth/Armstrong-Saurer

Sir W. G. Armstrong Whitworth & Co was a large industrial and engineering company based in Newcastle-upon-Tyne. It built its first commercial vehicles in 1906. These were bus chassis ordered by Motor Omnibus Construction of Walthamstow, a subsidiary of the London Motor Omnibus Co, which traded as Vanguard. Apparently, MOC could not take up all of its order, so those remaining were sold by Armstrong-Whitworth as lorries.

Some 25 years later Armstrong-Whitworth acquired the British manufacturing rights to the Swiss Saurer diesel-engined lorries, producing Armstrong-Saurer heavy lorries from 1931 onwards. There were also a few bodied as PSVs.

Below:
Placing the radiator behind the engine gave early Austins a distinctive appearance, shared only with Renault. This charabanc dates from about 1914. *Author's Collection*

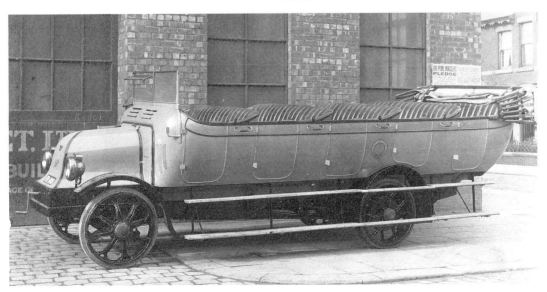

Atkinson

It was not until 1950 that Atkinson made its first purpose-designed diesel buses, but in 1924 it was said to be building a bus based on its four-ton steam wagon chassis, with upright boiler.

Austin

Austin was one of the most successful British car makers, and before World War 1 had added commercial vehicles to its range. A feature that easily distinguished them externally for some years was the coal-scuttle style bonnet: the radiator was mounted behind the engine with the fan being used to draw the air forward over the engine. Some 2,000 trucks went to the army in the war, numerous design changes being made in 1917. City of Oxford Tramways, the predecessor of City of Oxford Motor Services, bought 12 during the war, but the last had gone by the end of 1920. Austin had its own bus fleet (of Austins, of course) for transporting staff for some years.

The Russian Revolution resulted in the termination of an order placed by the murdered Czar's government, and many of these 2-3 ton models were slowly sold off until about 1922. Some, along with other ex-army Austins, were then bodied as buses and coaches. A smaller chassis, offered for a period in the early 1920s, was of more conventional design, but with the engine mounted over and forward of the front axle. Bodied as a 17-seat bus, with 'the great advantage of a four-speed gearbox' (a dig at the two-speed Ford T, no doubt), it cost £775 complete; electric light was an extra.

Subsequently the largest car chassis were occasionally bodied as small buses, but Austin did not reappear in the PSV market until 1939, when it announced the 'K' series goods and passenger models. Built in a new factory, the new semi-forward-control range had an overhead valve engine of 3,460cc, hydraulic brakes, synchromesh gearbox and an engine mounted far forward over the front axle. The whole design, even down to the shape of the radiator grille, was remarkably similar to the contemporary Bedford, and

some say only the outbreak of war prevented Bedford taking legal action. Few 'K'-types were built before production was switched to military requirements.

Auto-Mixte

For some six years this Belgian maker built petrol-electric chassis using the transmission designs of Henri Pieper, which were later also used in a Daimler bus. At least one Auto-Mixte chassis came to Britain. It was said to be the maker's first bus. Even by the standards of the day the chassis was remarkably high and bodybuilder E. & H. Hora designed and built, in 1906, a special body for it in just eight days. It was of a two-compartment type with high front compartment with steps and entrance doorway just ahead of the rear axle; the rear compartment was at a lower level and had an open-sided but roofed back in Paris bus style.

Auto-Traction

This Belgian maker set up in 1920, originally building a road tractor with Minerva engine. Pneumatic tyres were adopted quite early, and Minerva acquired the company in 1925. That year bodybuilder Waveney of Lowestoft was offering an Auto-Traction (normal-control, of course) fitted with 30-seat coach body with side access doors to each row of seats, sliding hood and rigid side curtains, and 12V lighting for £900 complete.

BACS

The British Automobile Construction Syndicate built a 32-seat open-top double-decker with 25hp Aster engine in 1910 for the London & North Western Railway, which used it on a route between Colwyn Bay and Old Colwyn.

Baico

Baico Patents was producing chassis extensions for commercial vehicles even in the 1920s. But from 1926 it also offered the Baico Boulevard Car, a small-wheel toastrack based on the Ford 1-ton chassis and intended for slow-speed summer running along seaside promenades. The first ran at Skegness. Baico added to the Ford a chassis extension, special outriggers and 24in (0.61m) diameter wheels with solid types. It seated 28 within its 20ft (6.09m) overall length.

Barton

The Barton brothers, later Barton Transport, were successful operators who in the 1920s went in for substantial rebuilding of chassis and later built their own. For a short time the company even designed and built its own four-cylinder diesel engine with monobloc aluminium casting; these were fitted in trucks and barges as well as Barton buses.

Early chassis conversion included lengthening various makes, and one Daimler 'Y'-type gained 10ft (3m) in length to become a 60-seat single-decker.

The company's forte was conversions to six-wheelers, often of unlikely chassis. A modest small Morris would emerge as a 24 or a 26-seat six-wheeler (and be known as a Morris-Barton); 12 or 14-seat Lancias became 26-seat vehicles on three axles; whilst a whole fleet of larger Lancias (many ex-Italian Government war surplus) appeared as 39 or 40-seat six-wheelers (Lancia-Bartons), usually with Barton's Gliders as fleetname.

Production of complete chassis began in 1929 with two chassis fitted with Meadows petrol engines. In 1930 there were 10 Bartons, five with Coventry Climax petrol engines, two with Gardner diesels, two with Continental Red Seal engines and one with a Sunbeam eight-cylinder petrol engine. Gearboxes and other mechanical parts also varied from chassis to chassis. Four chassis built in 1931 were fitted with Coventry Climax (one), Leyland petrol (one), Commer petrol (one) and Blackstone diesel (one) engines. The last-named was soon discarded. The final year, 1932, saw just two chassis, one with a Commer engine the other with a Barton diesel.

Barton had pioneered diesels after being impressed by a Gardner 4L2 at a shipping exhibition. In March 1930 it put into service one of its Lancia-Bartons with a 4L2, just days ahead of Sheffield Corporation's Karrier single-decker with Mercedes-Benz diesel. One of the two Bartons with Gardner diesels built in 1930 was of particular interest as it had the five-cylinder 5L2, the forerunner of the 5LW which was to become so successful.

New construction and use regulations on lengths, overhangs and other matters brought to an end the Barton lengthening and rebuilding schemes of the 1920s, while presumably the greater efficiency of Leyland and other commercial chassis of the early 1930s dissuaded Barton from more home building.

BAT

The initials stood for British Associated Transport. The chassis were made by Harris & Hasell (1929) Ltd of Bristol, whose predecessor had sold various makes for some years. It had done particularly well with US-built Reos. Perhaps reflecting the surge in patriotism in the depression, the company then designed and assembled two models of its own. The BAT Cruiser with six-cylinder engine was for up to 20 seats, whilst the BAT Super Pullman had an eight-cylinder engine for up to 32 seats. Cruisers sold quite well; one was even offered as a prize to the person suggesting the best improvement to the design. Competition and depression, however, meant that BAT lasted just two years.

Bean

The makers of the Bean were originally motor component manufacturers. For eight years they also produced commercial vehicle and bus chassis before ceasing business and reforming as component makers.

Below:
BAT's Cruiser was the smaller of the two models built, but boasted a six-cylinder engine. The model sold quite well and was offered as a basis for a 20-seat body. *Ian Allan Library*

Left:
Thomas Tilling's Brighton business bought four of these Beans at the end of 1926 and built 14-seat bodies for them. The 25cwt (1.25 ton) chassis had 14hp engines (as used in the Bean 14hp car) and worked well on hilly, rural routes, as one-man buses. They were replaced by 20-seat Dennis Darts in 1931-32. *Ian Allan Library*

From the mid-1920s the company's pneumatic-tyred normal-control buses with about 14 seats enjoyed a degree of popularity as 'handy little vehicles' and, unusually, were available with servo-assisted front-wheel brakes. For a short time there was also a heavier, forward-control model.

Beardmore

Most familiar as a maker of London-type taxis for many years, Beardmore was a Glasgow engineering company with diverse products including boilers and, at one stage, aircraft. The same four-cylinder engine as in the taxis was offered in conventional lorry chassis of ³/4 or 1¹/2 ton in the 1920s, and a number were bodied as buses. For lighter routes the Scottish Motor Traction Co bought nine with 15-seat bodies in 1925, but kept them only four years.

Beardmore was also a pioneer in developing 'heavy oil engines' as diesels were called in the 1930s. After trying one engine in a Leyland Titan, Glasgow Corporation ordered 30 for installation in a batch of 50 Albion Venturer double-deckers delivered in 1935; the other 20 had Gardner units. However, the Beardmore engines were not reliable and production ceased. Some of the Glasgow Albions later gained Leyland engines.

Beaufort

In the early years of this century the Beaufort Motor Co of Twickenham, Middlesex, built a few motor-buses. The firm is said to have had German connections and to have been formed to sell German-built vehicles in the UK. The London General Omnibus Co tried a couple of Beauforts at an early stage while the London & District Omnibus Co had one. All three were, of course, open-top double-deckers fitted with chain drive.

Bedford

The Bedford story is a relatively simple and successful one. The American-owned manufacturer, which had been assembling Chevrolets in this country, went one step further and commenced UK production, partly to avoid import duties. It kept the model range simple, sold at competitive prices and used a talented designer. Bedford production began in 1931 and, by 1939, the company claimed that 70% of buses and coaches with less than 26 seats on British roads were Bedfords.

The first models built were goods vehicles, with two bus model derivatives with low-framed chassis following in August 1931: the WHB for 14-seat bodies and the WLB for 20-seats. The WHB had a relatively short run, being dropped in mid-1933. They were all built in the Vauxhall factory at Luton, Bedfordshire, that previously had assembled Chevrolets and recent comparisons of preserved makes from the 1930s have revealed that some Chevrolet components were used in early Bedfords.

The 1933 Motor Show saw a new 3-ton truck model unveiled. It was of semi-forward-control layout with a short bonnet and was designed by Stepney Acres. By 1935 there was a PSV derivative, the WTL. It was replaced in 1936 by the WTB, a more purpose-built chassis with a longer wheelbase. It offered space for six more seats, and its popularity soon grew, with Duple having a long and successful collaboration with

Right:
The earliest Bedford PSVs were quite small, two models generally seating 14 or 20, although lack of demand gave the smaller of the two a short life. It was, however, a useful vehicle on Scottish islands and in other rural areas. *Author's Collection*

Below:
Walter Alexander & Sons both bodied and operated this 20-seat WLB of 1934. It carries the short-lived Royal Blue Coaches fleet-name. Note the small destination display above the registration plate. *Ian Allan Library*

Above:
Bedfords really came into their own from the mid-1930s with the semi-forward-control layout which gave room for up to 26 seats. A coach version, folding roof opened, touts for trade on the front at Swanage. *Author's Collection*

Left:
This Willmott 26-seat coach body, based on a 1937 WTB chassis, was supplied to Eugene, pioneers of home perms for ladies. The coach (and three others) carried Eugene Mermaids, ladies who gave hair perming demonstrations. *Author's Collection*

Left:
The open bonnet of this 1942 OWB (described at the time as a Ministry of Supply single-decker) shows the easy accessibility of carburettor, filter, air cleaner, fuse box and dynamo. An engine-driven tyre pump was a standard fitment. *Author's Collection*

Bedford. Duple offered some nine body versions for the type. Brakes were servo-assisted.

One other major change came in the summer of 1938: an improved engine giving 72bhp against the 64bhp of the old one. The successor, unveiled in 1939, was the OB, designed for up to 29-seat bodies, with a slightly longer wheelbase but with the same engine. Just 73 were built before war intervened, though production restarted after the war. But for hard-pressed operators the Ministry of Supply authorised production from 1942 onwards of a utility version — the OWB. It was the only new single-decker available, and came only with a petrol engine. Despite this, many went to larger operators who, by that time, had standardised on diesel-engined vehicles. Mention should also be made of a factory-built seven-seater rural bus (a conversion of the 7cwt [350kg] van) which was in production from 1932 to 1939.

The OWB was the most successful chassis in production terms, with 3,398 built. In comparison there were 2,320 WTBs and 1,895 WLBs. The short (and shortlived) WHB totalled just 102. All the figures, except the OWB, include chassis built for export.

Strangely, the earliest Bedford coaches sold were based on goods chassis; Bedford generally commenced production of goods models first. Some bodybuilders and operators couldn't wait! By July 1931 Jennings of Sandbach (better known as a truck bodybuilder) was offering a 20-seater with canvas roof, while Waveney of Oulton Broad, near Lowestoft, offered a fixed-roof 20-seater. Both were probably beaten by Rainford of Lincoln, which delivered a 20-seater to a small Lincolnshire operator in August 1931. Waveney followed with a 14-seater on a proper drop frame PSV chassis at the end of that month, the first true Bedford PSV. Early in 1935 Duple and others were offering coach bodies on the new WT truck chassis introduced well before its WTB companion.

Belhaven

Belhaven built steam and petrol-engined vehicles for a number of years at Wishaw, Lanarkshire. An early Belhaven steam bus ran between Glasgow and Eaglesham for a time, and the first two buses in the fleet of Walter Alexander were Belhavens, one built in 1914 and the other in 1916. Production ceased in 1924.

Bellis & Morcom

Birmingham-based Bellis & Morcom was an established company producing mainly stationary steam engines. It built just one bus, a double-decker. The London General Omnibus Co ran the bus from the end of 1907 to the autumn of 1908 on three different routes. The bus had twin chain final drive.

Belsize

Belsize Motors of Manchester built its first commercial vehicle in 1906, after having built cars successfully since 1901. A shaft-driven three-ton truck with 28hp four-cylinder engine was introduced in 1911. This was also offered as a charabanc. Not all wartime

Below:
Belsize enjoyed brief success as a bus builder in World War 1 — when other makes were not available. British Automobile Traction, the BET subsidiary, bought a number for some of its operations. BAT buses ran under the 'British' fleetname in a number of areas before individually named subsidiaries were established. *Geoff Lumb Collection*

production went for military use, so British Automobile Traction (a subsidiary of British Electric Traction) bought a considerable number. Some of those acquired ran in the Thames Valley, becoming part of the fleet of Thames Valley Traction Co when that company was formed in 1920. Scottish General Transport, forerunner of Western SMT, ran seven, all acquired in 1915 or 1916.

Berliet

Not many Berliets were sold in the UK, although the maker became France's largest builder of commercial vehicles before, more recently, being swallowed by Renault. An early British buyer was Bristol Tramways, which ordered three in 1907; they were not delivered until 1909 and were open-toppers with the driver seated far forward above the engine.

An operator of smaller, later, single-deck Berliets was Westcliff Motor Services (later to be merged with Eastern National), which ran six pneumatic-tyred examples in the 1920s.

A notable feature of a new medium-sized four-wheeler with four-cylinder engine introduced in 1924 was its brakes. 'Exceptionally large brake drums' on the twin rear wheels were 'brought into use by the hand lever, while the pedal brake (also of the internal-expanding type) was drum-mounted behind the gearbox on the second motion shaft.' There were front brakes too, and these could, as an extra, be interconnected with the transmission brake. *Motor Transport* of the time thought this feature could be of particular value to coach owners in the hilly districts of Wales, Scotland and the West Country, where accidents due to insufficient and inefficient braking were still all too frequent.

Berna

Sales of foreign chassis in the UK seemed to increase in the years just before World War 1. One of the more successful was the Swiss Berna company, although it had a chequered career. It began exporting to Britain in 1906, but got into difficulties. These resulted in an English financial group, Hudson Consolidated, taking over and continuing the business. The success of the range improved, and in 1912 a Swiss consortium bought the company back. An English company handled sales in Britain, but 1914 saw a surprising development with the formation of a rival — British Berna Motor Lorries of Guildford. In the mid-1920s the normal-control chassis was offered as a 25-seat bus, 30-seat 'open coach', or even a 58-seat double-deck bus.

Bethlehem

The American steel company of this name built commercial vehicles for some 10 years with very mixed fortunes. One year saw production totalling 3,500, while a little later it had fallen to less than one a week. Some chassis were exported, and at one stage a number were assembled by the Scottish Motor Traction Co.

Blackburn

A. Blackburn & Co of Cleckheaton, Yorkshire, built 10hp two-cylinder and 20hp four-cylinder chassis for two or three years up to 1908. A number were bodied as 12-seater charabancs.

BMMO

Midland Red's path into bus manufacture began before 1923, when it built its first complete chassis. For a few years it had followed a policy of having replacement parts for the Tilling-Stevens vehicles in the fleet made to its own design by local engineering companies. Though the parts were often more expensive, the higher quality was found to be more economical in the long run.

By 1940 Midland Red had built over 2,000 chassis, of which just under half were sold to associated companies, including Ortona Motor Co and Peterborough Electric Traction (both later part of Eastern Counties), Northern General (and its sister companies), Potteries and Trent. All these chassis were known by the generic designation of SOS, which stood for Shire's Omnibus Specification. L. G. Wyndham Shire was the talented chief engineer who persuaded the company that it should build its own vehicles. Some competitors were at the time able to run rings around the company's larger, solid-tyred and ponderous buses by using small, fast lightweight buses on pneumatic tyres.

The first year of production saw three prototypes followed by 19 production models. These and the larger output in 1924 were all built on Tilling-Stevens frames, but transmission was orthodox, with four-speed gearbox. The engine was a 4.3 litre petrol unit with four cylinders and side valves. This benefited from advice by Harry Ricardo, who was later famed for his diesel expertise. The engine had high compression ratio and relatively high output. All the vehicles had pneumatic tyres. One of the hallmarks of the design was its light weight, which was helped by the maker knowing exactly what body (in style and weight) was to be put on the chassis.

From 1925 the whole chassis was of Midland Red design, and by 1926 the company had moved to forward-control models. More design changes the following year produced the 'Q'-type, on which the wheelbase was lengthened and the bonnet shortened. The cab was moved further forward, but shifting the engine and radiator slightly to the nearside improved cab space. The offset position of the radiator gave these and subsequent Midland Red vehicles an even more distinctive appearance, something that was enhanced on single-deckers by the use of destination boards instead of blinds. The changes gave the 'Q'-type a seating capacity of 37.

Right:
Many early bonneted SOS buses lost their original bodies to older chassis in 1929-30 and gained new ones of slightly lower capacity built by United Auto Services at Lowestoft. The chassis of this one had been new in 1925, and was photographed in 1949 in use as a tree cutter. *C. D. Wilkinson*

Top:
The narrow offset cab and absence of destination blind boxes gave the SOS single-deckers a unique appearance. Many went to other operators; this one is seen in later life with a subsidiary of Northern General. *Ian Allan Library*

Above:
BMMO had continued with normal-control layout for some years for charabancs. Later models had six-cylinder engines, including this 1930 QLC with Short 29-seat body seen on an extended tour of Devon, crossing the river at Kingsbridge. It was one of a batch of 18. *Author's Collection*

Developments in design came thick and fast over the next few years, with the 'QL' in 1928 with four-wheel brakes and twin rear wheels to permit a lower frame height, and the 'M' (for Madam) type in 1929 with more comfortable and fewer (34) seats to attract ladies going shopping to use the buses. Later versions were the IM4 and IM6 (the latter fitted with a six-cylinder engine), of which nearly 400 were built.

The years 1929 and 1930 saw a wealth of different types produced, and by 1934 there were four different designs of six-cylinder engine in the fleet. Strangely, there had been no double-deckers left in the fleet since 1929, but traffic growth, and maybe sheer economics, brought a prototype in 1931, followed by 50 production models in 1932-33. They eventually became known as REDDs (rear-entrance double-deckers). Another prototype, with front entrance (FEDD), came in 1933, and was followed by 50 production models in 1934. A further 135 in 1935-36 had Metro-Cammell all-metal bodies that proved remarkably durable. Surprisingly, all were petrol-engined, but the Metro-Cammell-bodied examples were converted to diesel from 1942 onwards, with a mixture of AEC 7.7 litre and BMMO's own engines being fitted. Another 150 FEDDs with diesel engines followed in 1938-39. Three had full fronts, which were later removed, but in 1942 a full-width front and concealed radiator along with restyled upper-deck front were fitted to an FEDD. It was followed by an elegant prototype postwar double-decker in 1945. This had four-bay bodywork, sliding window vents, radiused windows and full-width bonnet and concealed radiator. Its appearance set the standard for Midland Red and others for many years.

The company seemed to have mixed views on coach design. It had continued to build batches of normal-control charabancs up to 1930, the last having six-cylinder engines. It went back to normal control with a new style of touring coach in 1935, the OLR (open low Rolls-Royce). They had long bonnets and canvas roofs. More-or-less contemporary with this dated style were what might be termed the ordinary coaches, the LRRs (low Rolls-Royce) of 1934-35 which were forward-control half-cabs of rather peculiar appearance; the roof canopy was not extended over the bonnet, but the driver's cab had its windscreen and side windows at a noticeably higher level than the side windows on the rest of the coach.

Of course, the company did not get everything right first time. The first enclosed coaches (for long-distance work, not touring) were the 'XLs' (Excel) of 1929-30. However, the lightweight chassis, despite the six-cylinder engines, could not cope with the extra weight. So new chassis, the 'RR' (Rolls-Royce), were built for them, bus bodies being fitted to the 'XL' chassis. Even stranger was a batch of normal-control buses produced in 1929 for quieter routes. Their chassis were early bonneted 'SOSs', whose bodies went on surviving Tilling-Stevens buses. Fifty new normal-control 26-seat bodies were built by United at its Lowestoft, Suffolk, works — which later became ECW — and a further 33 conversions were carried out for Trent, Llandudno Blue (a company later to become part of Crosville) and Ortona. The new vehicles were designated as 'ODD'. After 1934, incidentally, Trent was the only other company to continue buying Midland Red chassis.

Coaches of a rather better appearance were the 50 SLRs (saloon low Rolls-Royce) of 1937, which were forward-control vehicles with English Electric full-fronted bodywork with concealed radiators. Surprisingly, they were built with petrol engines, but gained Leyland 7.4 litre diesel engines postwar. The first diesel-engined coaches were the ONCs of 1939, with full-fronted concealed radiator bodies by Duple. They had five-speed gearboxes.

A new range of single-deck bus introduced in 1934 was the ON (Onward) which took advantage of the recently introduced longer length limit of 27ft 6in for single-deckers and squeezed in 38 seats. Some with diesel engines followed (seating only 36) but then Midland Red designed its own 8 litre 'K' series engine, which was shorter and seating capacity was thus increased again to 38. From 1936 to 1940 the 'SON' (Saloon Onward) was standard. It also had Midland Red's 'K'-type 8 litre diesel engine. One strange feature of virtually all Midland Red's single-deck buses was the absence of roller destination blinds; the company continued to use destination boards and route number stencils.

Among the more significant vehicles were four rear-engined single-deck prototypes (three buses and one coach) built in 1935-36. These had petrol engines mounted transversely across the rear, and hydraulic throttle operation. Initially, two of the vehicles had fluid flywheels and epicyclic gearboxes. All had set-back front axles, with the entrance ahead of the axle on the three buses.

One failing discovered in operation over a period was the ingesting of dust by the engine, which caused considerable wear. However, during the war they were rebuilt by Midland Red's relatively new and innovative chief engineer, Donald Sinclair. The main change was the removal of the engine from the rear, and its replacement by a new horizontal version of the company's own 8 litre 'K'-type diesel. Experience with the buses in their new form enabled Midland Red to be the first manufacturer to put this layout into full production after 1945.

Left:
A typical mid-1930s double-decker, this FEDD dates from 1936 and has a Metro-Cammell all-metal body of a type that was to prove particularly durable. The fuel tank under the driver's seat is a typical BMMO feature. All the batch of 135 later gained AEC or BMMO diesel engines. *Ian Allan Library*

Left:
Duple bodied a batch of 25 ONC coaches in 1939. These were the first coaches built with diesel engines, and also had five-speed gearboxes. Like a previous batch of coaches built in 1937, they had full fronts and centre entrances. This one is seen in Banbury. *Author*

Brillie

Frenchman Eugene Brillie designed and had built by the Schneider company a range of commercial vehicles and buses for about four years before going bankrupt. As on other French buses, the driver was seated above the engine. The Star horsebus concern of Solomon Andrews in London began running motorbuses in 1905. The company tried a few makes before settling on the Brillie and buying 15. However, Star could not make motorbuses pay and withdrew its motorbus fleet in 1907, reverting entirely to horse traction.

Bristol

Bristol was another of the small band of early motorbus operators which found the chassis it bought to be less than satisfactory and decided as a result to built its own. The company came into being in 1874

Above right:
Bristol Tramways built and operated this design of 'composite charabanc' at Weston-super-Mare before World War 1. It could seat 20, or 22 passengers 'with centre seat' — presumably a reference to the two seats alongside the driver. *Author's Collection*

Right:
After World War 1 Bristol resumed production with the new 4-ton chassis with worm drive and 40hp Bristol engine. Kingston-upon-Hull Corporation was the buyer of this 1923 example, with body by tramcar builder Dick Kerr of Preston. *Ian Allan Library*

Below:
Bristol described its four-cylinder engined 'B'-type of 1926 as a 'light passenger model' though it was also know as the Superbus. It sold well, and widely, usually as about a 30-seater. But this was one of two built in 1930 for Stockton-on-Tees Corporation as 26-seat one-man buses. *Ian Allan Library*

Left:
Underneath the new body and lowered radiator of this 1949 product was supposed to be the chassis of a 1930 Bristol 'B'. One of a number reconstructed by Bristol at a time when there were restrictions on supplying new buses to the home market, it probably contained a few token original parts (and the original registration number), but really was a way of obtaining more new vehicles. *Ian Allan Library*

Left:
Bristol's 'G'-type was introduced in 1932 as a double-decker, alongside 'H' and 'J' single-deckers. Initially fitted with Bristol's six-cylinder petrol engine, it was soon offered with a variety of diesel engines. Most popular was the Gardner five-cylinder, as on this 1935 example for the company's own fleet. *Ian Allan Library*

Right:
The 'K'-type double-decker of 1937 had a lower frame and other improvements. The onset of war eventually stopped production, but there were unfrozen examples. Production resumed in 1944 in utility form, initially fitted with the AEC 7.7 litre engine. Illustrated is one built for Merthyr Tydfil Corporation, which is pictured in 1963 when its Park Royal body had been somewhat rebuilt. *K. Bateman*

as the Bristol Tramways Co and in 1887 was retitled the Bristol Tramways & Carriage Co after a merger. Its horse-drawn trams were replaced by electric ones in 1895 and the company also ran horse buses and horse-drawn cabs. It began running buses in 1906 with Thornycrofts with Berliets and Fiats, soon following, but was unhappy with them; indeed the company won a legal action against the Fiat supplier.

Bristol began building its own chassis and engines in 1908, when it produced five normal-control chain-driven vehicles of type C40. These lasted until the early 1920s and were said to be an improved version of the Thornycrofts. More followed until 1911, when a slightly larger version was introduced. The Filton works where they were built was shared with sister company Bristol Aeroplane, and to give more space for building aircraft bus construction was moved to the Brislington Motor Construction Works (as it was called). By early 1915 a total of over 120 chassis had been built. First to be sold to another operator went to Imperial Tramways (Middlesbrough) in 1914, a company in which Bristol had a financial interest.

Bus chassis building ceased in 1915 and the factory turned to war work on Bristol aircraft. Building resumed in 1920, the year in which the company took a stand at the Olympia Motor Show for the first time, with a new model. This was the four-tonner, with Bristol 40hp engine, which was sold as either a bus or a truck. Bus production ended in 1927, though goods models continued for a time. All told, some 650 were built. These were bodied by outside builders as well as Bristol itself. They were sold to many operators. All bar nine were single-deck; the double-deckers went to Hull Corporation in 1923. That year saw the Bristol range widened with the introduction of the two-ton model. This was a forward-control chassis usually seating around 20. Its production ran for six years and of the 250 built over half went into the Bristol bus operating fleet.

Replacement of the four-tonner came as the 'A'-type, a low-frame heavyweight chassis that sold in small numbers mainly to municipal fleets. Much more successful was the 'B'-type or Superbus of 1926. A lightweight, with 75bhp Bristol engine, it was built until 1934 and totalled nearly 780 including 300 for Bristol's own fleet. Another big operator was United Automobile Services and several municipalities also bought the type. A similar chassis was called the 'D'-type; this had Bristol's six-cylinder JW engine.

Three new models came in 1931: the 'G'-type double-decker; and the 'H' and 'J'-type single-deckers. The 'G' and 'J' had the six-cylinder engine, the 'H' the four. These were all petrol engines, but it was not long before various diesel engines — from AEC, Beardmore, Dennis, Gardner and Leyland — were being tried. Large numbers of Gardner engines were subsequently fitted, though some Js from Bristol's own coach fleet had AEC diesel engines, while Dennis four-cylinder diesels were fitted in

buses for Bristol's Gloucester subsidiary and for Eastern Counties. 'Gs' and 'Js' remained in production until 1937, by which time nearly 250 'Gs' and well over 800 'Js' had been built. 'Hs' were less popular and their production ended earlier. These high production figures reflected the 1931 incorporation of the company into the Tilling Group, and its subsequent development as a main supplier to other operators in the group, effectively filling the gap left by Tilling-Stevens and TSM. For this Bristol had to enlarge its Brislington premises.

The design of the 'Gs' and 'Js' was becoming somewhat dated, with the gearbox mounted separately amidships, while frame height was greater than most other makes. This meant that 'Gs' with low-height bodywork were rather higher than, say, a Leyland Titan with a similar body. On the other hand, the option of a five-speed gearbox on the 'J' was well ahead of other makes. The rigid mounting of the Gardner engines — particularly five-cylinder ones — on chassis built from 1936 transmitted noise and vibration through the whole vehicle, but surprisingly this feature was continued on the otherwise much more modern 'K' double-deck and 'L' single-deck chassis introduced in the latter part of 1937. By now there were no petrol engine options, and both had the 5LW as standard with the 6LW as an option. Some single-deckers for operators with easy terrain even had 4LWs. The gearbox was new, but again offered in four-speed or overdrive five-speed form.

Wartime work at Brislington consisted of production of aircraft components, armaments and other defence items, but in addition nearly 2,500 anthracite-burning trailers were built to some six different designs. These were the result of a Government initiative to reduce reliance on scarce imported fuels, and were generally used with petrol-engined buses. They consumed a home-produced fuel, but were troublesome and reduced engine life as well. Bristol also built two 'L'-types with the gas producer built into the bodywork in a fireproof compartment at the offside rear of the vehicle. The national shortage of buses led to Bristol restarting bus production in 1944, with an austerity version of the 'K'-type. However, almost all of these were fitted with the AEC 7.7 litre engine since Gardners (as used in Guy chassis) were in very short supply.

British and Brush

The British Electric Traction Co was originally a tramway operator. However, it soon saw the potential of the motorbus, buying two Straker-Squire steam buses in 1901 and putting them to work with subsidiary Potteries Electric Traction Co. The duo did not last long, however. Another attempt at bus operation in 1904 saw PET receive three Brush-built double-deckers fitted with Mutel petrol engines, but two only lasted two years.

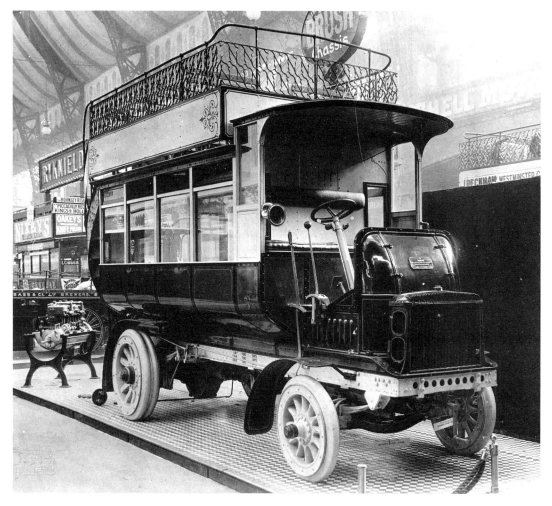

Above:
The Amalgamated Motor Bus Co of London had been promoted by British Automobile Development, a BET subsidiary, with the dream of running 120 motorbuses in London as replacements for 180 horse-buses. But all that transpired, between 1907 and 1908, was five of these buses of Brush manufacture. *Author's Collection*

Right:
Six of the nine Brush 'B'-types bought by BMMO between October 1906 and January 1907 moved south after the company abandoned motorbus operation, and formed the fleet of Deal & District Motor Services in 1908. They were still, however, owned by BMMO. This one was claimed to be the first front-entrance motorbus. *Ian Allan Library*

What had been BET's automobile committee became in 1905 the British Automobile Development Co, with powers of making, selling, hiring or promoting the operation of buses. Alongside BET's Brush tramcar works at Loughborough a separate assembly plant was erected. Brush built both chassis and body, some to a driver-over-engine design, with engines coming from either Peter Brotherhood or Daimler. BAD became British Automobile Traction Co in 1910.

Early buses had been badged British, but the name soon changed to Brush. The exhibit at the company's stand at what was said to be the first Commercial Motor Exhibition in 1907 was claimed to be the first bus with an all-metal body. Five Brush double-deckers were put into service by the Amalgamated Omnibus Co on a route between London's Oxford Circus and Peckham in 1907 and 1908, but all had gone by the end of 1908. Midland Red bought a number of Brush buses, and six quite new ones went to Deal & District Motor Services after Midland Red gave up motorbus operation in November 1907.

British Berna

Swiss Berna chassis had been sold in the UK for some years and, for a time, the Swiss company was owned by a British financial group. However, a surprise to many was the formation in 1914 of a rival — British Berna Motor Lorries of Guildford. The products were similar and were made in Newcastle-upon-Tyne by the engineering and casting company Henry Watson & Sons. Soon after the end of World War 1, Henry Watson & Sons announced a range of its own chassis, which were sold under its own name.

British Ensign

Beginning as Ensign Motors in southwest London in 1913, the company soon added the prefix British to its title. By 1914 it had added commercial vehicle chassis to its range. These had Tylor engines. Some chassis built after the war were fitted with Dorman engines. One British Ensign was bodied as a chara-banc by Carmichaels of Worcester for local operator Burnham. Southdown was a surprising buyer of the make, in 1915, acquiring a number along with some from other obscure manufacturers. An early buyer of Ensigns was another southeast operator, Strong's Garage & Motor Car Co of Margate, which had five.

Brockway

Brockway became one of the largest of the American truck builders and during the late 1920s a number of its chassis were imported into the UK by agent A. E. Tapper & Co. The chassis had a six-cylinder petrol engine and was of normal-control layout, with pneumatic tyres. They were suitable for bodies seating from 14 to 32 passengers.

BSA

BSA stood for Birmingham Small Arms Co, a company better known in the automotive field for its motorbikes and cars and for its ownership of Daimler. It made occasional ventures into the van market but its large car chassis were sometimes used as the basis of small buses. A notable example of this was a 12-seater BSA bus bought by Haslingden Corporation in 1919. The bus was impossibly unreliable and lasted less than a year, being replaced by an Austin 22-seater. But the BSA has a possible claim to fame as it was designed and built as a one-man bus with a front entrance alongside the driver and is said by some to be the country's first proper OMO vehicle.

Burford

Burford enjoyed considerable success with the Great Western Railway for a time, supplying over 70 small buses, some of which were later converted to GWR goods vehicles. National Omnibus & Transport was the other big customer, not altogether surprising considering that H. G. Burford was also a director. H. G. Burford had been the founder of Milnes-Daimler. In 1914 he began importing an American chassis which was sold under the Burford name. Later the chassis gained a greater British content.

By 1921 a chassis was offered with four-wheel brakes. Burford and the GWR apparently collaborated in developing semi-forward-control and forward-control models seating 16-18, an unusual feature at this time for small vehicles. Although intended for passenger carrying, most models were known by their weight capacity. Burford went into liquidation in the mid-1920s, but was bought out by its general manager who continued the business on a small scale.

Plymouth Corporation had quite a fleet of Burfords by the late 1920s, having bought two batches of 10 after an initial three. All were 'B'-type 50cwt (2 1/2 ton or 2,540kg) bonneted 20-seaters which were one-man operated.

Bussing

This well-known and longlived German maker of buses and trucks began production in 1903, had built its first bus chassis in 1904, and, it is believed, began selling them to the UK in the same year. Certainly the rights to UK sales were acquired by an old-established Bristol engineering company in 1905, which reformed itself as Sidney Straker & Squire. Within a year the company had to move to a larger factory. The original 24hp model was followed by 34hp and 40hp models. All had chain drive and a radiator mounted low down at the front. By the time of the merger of the big three motorbus operators in London into the LGOC in 1908 there were over 350 Straker-Squires running in the capital. Straker & Squire went on to develop its own chassis designs, which are described in the entry under its name. The London Road Car Co, fleetname Vanguard, had tried a Bussing early on, before later standardising on Straker-Squires, while the LGOC had nearly 60 Bussings as well as Straker-Squires.

Many years later German-built Bussings were offered on the British market, in the shape of a normal-control 32-seater.

Caledon

Scottish Commercial Cars of Glasgow had happily handled sales of Commers for some years, only to find the supply ceasing when World War 1 broke out. The company then made the courageous decision to design and build its own vehicle. Caledon was the name chosen and production started in 1915. Dorman engines and a French design of gearbox were fitted to a very substantial chassis. Sales built up, and some of the crudities of the early chassis were eliminated. After the war the maker became the separate company, Caledon Motors, and, lured on by high sales in 1919, not only widened the range considerably, but also designed and built its own sleeve-valve engines — a costly exercise. Not many chassis with this engine were sold, though two PSV exhibits at the 1921 Olympia Show had them, together with pneumatic tyres and, in one case, electric lighting. These were quite advanced additions to what was a rather basic design.

But hard times meant that production stopped in 1922, only for it to be restarted by SCC, albeit in small numbers. Production continued haltingly until 1926 when Caledon was acquired by steam lorry builder Garretts of Leiston (Suffolk). Thereafter no more buses were made. Total Caledon production was little more than 700, with probably a modest proportion of these for passenger use, but there was at least one double-decker. However, during World War 1 there were some surprising customers, such as Southdown. Postwar adverts offered chain-driven

chassis in a number of capacities for goods as well as a 40hp chassis with live axle for passengers.

Charron

This French car maker diversified briefly into the production of a luxury single-deck 'Pullman' chassis with 30hp engine, chain drive and pneumatic tyres. The General Motor Co put some into service in London during 1908, but they do not seem to have lasted long.

Chelmsford and Clarkson

Thomas Clarkson was a Lancastrian and an inventor, who was continually innovating and improving his product — steam buses. He built and ran more than anybody else and, when that era ended, went off to design an improved steam lorry. The earliest buses were called Chelmsford, after the Essex town where they were made, but later ones carried the Clarkson name.

Several early vehicles worked in Torquay, and two Chelmsfords ran for the Sussex Motor Road Car Co between Worthing and Pulborough in 1904. Road Car, before its merger with the LGOC, built up a fleet of over 70, and in 1909 the LGOC's Frank Searle encouraged Clarkson to convert one of its De Dions to steam propulsion. However, the LGOC then began withdrawing its steam fleet so Clarkson, with the backing of friends, formed his own company, the National Steam Car Co, to take over the factory and build and run steam buses. By 1914 it had 173 in London and others in Chelmsford. All the London examples had to meet the demanding unladen weight limit of $3^{1}/_{2}$ tons brought in by the Metropolitan Police Regulations of 1909.

Unfortunately, by the end of the war, labour costs had increased considerably, there were spares problems and the fuel (naphtha or paraffin) at one stage rose 2,700% in cost. An arrangement with the LGOC saw the last withdrawn in November 1919 and National taking over LGOC's Bedford outpost. One of the most colourful aspects of London bus operation had gone.

Chevrolet

The Chevrolet Motor Co was a division of General Motors, and added one-ton commercials to its car production at the end of World War 1. The first were sold in Britain in 1923 and sales soon built up. GM

Left:
The narrow rear track of this Chevrolet bus cannot have helped stability, even if it was on pneumatic tyres. Most sold in the UK gained bodies seating about 14, though there were some seven-seaters. *Ian Allan Library*

gained control of English car maker Vauxhall in 1925 and from 1928 Vauxhall also built Chevrolet commercials at Luton. A typical transatlantic sales gimmick of the late 1920s was the new range with 3.2 litre six-cylinder 'Cast Iron Wonder' engine — 'a six for the price of a four'. Chevrolet production at Luton was phased out in 1931 as building of the new Bedford got under way; there was some carry-over of components.

Citroen

Well-known French car and commercial vehicle maker Citroen built up a range of products that might be compared with those of Morris and Morris-Commercial together. It offered normal-control chassis for PSV use in the UK for a few years up to 1933. At one time there was a 1³/4-ton chassis for up to 14 seats, and later a larger chassis for 20-seaters.

Clement-Bayard

It seems appropriate that the Guernsey Railway Co should have operated a 14-seat bus on this French-built chassis; the railway also ran three Brillie double-deckers. But all four were imported from England secondhand. Vans, trucks and charabancs were built by this company up to 1914, but those sold in the UK appear to have been smaller chassis, taking bodies with up to 14 seats.

Clyde

Mackay & Jardine of Wishaw, Lanarkshire, built Clyde chassis for a number of years. Both men had previously worked for Belhaven, which was also in the same locality. The products of smaller makers, such as Clyde, generally sold to smaller operators, and these were a diminishing species by the early 1930s. Despite this, the make was still listed until the late 1930s. Unusually, the company built its own gearboxes. Examples of the Clyde, which was a normal-control chassis, could be found in the Walter Alexander and Central SMT fleets. All had been acquired when smaller operators had been bought out.

Commer

This company began as Commercial Cars in 1905 and its first chassis was developed around a gearbox. The gearbox was the Lindley, a kind of pre-selector developed by an engineer who had seen the difficulties drivers had with early gearboxes, and the damage they caused to the boxes. In Lindley's design, movement of the 'gear' level positioned dog clutches, which subsequently sprang into position when the clutch was depressed. A consortium originally formed to build a prototype gearbox for test ended up designing a chassis to go with it. The combination

Above:
Commer built double-deckers from the earliest days. The picture of this well-loaded example shows the poor state of many roads, even in towns, in the earliest years of this century. *Geoff Lumb Collection*

was successful, Commercial Cars was formed and it soon moved from a small south London workshop to a new factory at Luton.

By 1907 the company was offering passenger-carrying chassis and the first double-decker followed in 1909. As well as PSV models there was also the Norfolk Convertible Country House and Estate Car, which received 'numerous testimonials from notable users'. It was an omnibus, a shooting brake or an estate lorry. For use as a shooting brake it had gun racks and cartridge lockers, while as an omnibus it could carry up to 14 passengers and about ³/4 ton (750kg) of their luggage. Sales of chassis greatly increased in the years just before World War 1, to such an extent that Dorman built engines for some vehicles to the design of Commercial Cars, and other help was provided by Hillman. An advanced passenger model, the 3P, with 'live' rear axle instead of the chain drive previously used, was about to be introduced when war broke out and so did not go on sale until 1919. Wartime production peaked at 640 four-ton trucks in 1916.

As new models were introduced in the 1920s, the Lindley gearbox was gradually phased out, ceasing to be fitted after 1926. The passenger model for 20 or 30 seats (on two different wheelbases) was the 2P, designed for pneumatic tyres on both axles. The model later gained an engine with plain bearings (as opposed to roller), becoming the 4PW, and later a forward-control version, the 4PF, was added. Pressure lubrication was another feature of the engine.

The postwar slump had hit the company hard and from 1922 it had been run by a receiver and manager. In 1926 the company was sold to Humber of

Above:
No fewer than 29 passengers could apparently be seated in this Commer demonstrator shown at the 1922 Scottish Motor Show. The 3P worm-drive chassis had 'an electric lighting set' and — unusually for the time — pneumatic tyres all round. *Author's Collection*

Left:
The operator of this Commer PLNF5, delivered in 1939, was MacDougall's Motor Excursion Tours of Oban. The vehicle's Waveney body (a make popular on Commers) had two-and-one seating. *Author's Collection*

Coventry, which changed the name to Commer Cars and then reduced prices. Passenger models with Humber engines were offered from 1927 as both four and six-wheelers, seating up to 32.

A further takeover in 1928 placed Commer as part of Rootes Securities. The next year saw the introduction of a new, light 20-seater, the Invader, which used a modified version of the Humber six-cylinder Snipe engine. The gearbox was mounted in unit with it, and had 'silent third' helical gears. A new and bigger six-cylinder engine developed at Luton and producing 105bhp was fitted in a larger new model, the Avenger, for 32-seat single-deck or 50-seat double-deck bodies. However, from the mid-1930s Commer offered only 20 or 26-seat models, the former only with normal control.

In 1939 came the new Superpoise series for a whole range of goods and passenger applications. It had in the one design 'the time-tested virtues of both normal and forward control'; in other words, it was of semi-forward control layout. Both diesel and petrol engines were offered, with a choice of wheelbases to provide from 20 to 32 seats.

Cottin Desgouttes

Shaft drive was an early feature of trucks built by French maker Cottin Desgouttes. This company was best known for its well-made, durable and attractive cars. Buses, when introduced, became popular with French municipal operators, and a few chassis with charabanc bodies of capacities between 20 and 26 operated in two Scottish independent fleets that were later taken over by Scottish Motor Traction in the mid to late 1920s.

Cremorne

Chelsea-based Cremorne built some steam vehicles between about 1903 and 1906, including cars and commercial vehicles. One c.v. chassis fitted with a horsebus body was tried in London by the Associated Omnibus Co in 1905, but found to be too lightly built. There was also a purpose-built 36-seat steam bus with kerosene-fired vertical boiler.

Critchley-Norris

Bamber Bridge is a small town just a few miles from Preston (where Atkinsons were made) and from Leyland (Leylands); for three years the town boasted its own motor manufacturer — Critchley-Norris. J. S. Critchley designed the vehicles, which were fitted (like contemporary Leylands) with Crossley petrol engines — he had previously worked for Crossley.

Across in Yorkshire, Todmorden Corporation had planned to operate trams but had been discouraged by the cost and opted for buses instead. Bus services

Above:
Widnes Corporation bought four complete double-deckers in 1909; delivery from Luton was a four-day journey, partly because they were covered-top double-deckers. They were the first covered-top double-deckers to run regularly in Great Britain. Widnes had a corrosive atmosphere from its factories, which meant that, when it rained, the resulting precipitation was mildly acidic. It is believed that this was the reason for specifying roofs. *Geoff Lumb Collection*

Below:
Despite building for only three years, Critchley-Norris managed to spread its few vehicles to a number of towns. This one, with customary admirers as well as passengers, was said to be the first motorbus in Widnes. *Geoff Lumb Collection*

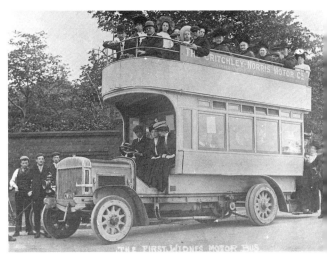

Left:
Secondhand Crossley 20/25s were popular small buses in the early 1920s. In the northeast, Northern General had six as 14-seaters, while this one, with an independent running from Rothbury to Newcastle-upon-Tyne, proved more successful than most in coping with the wintry weather of 1921-22. *Author's Collection*

began on 1 January 1907 with one double-deck and one single-deck Critchley-Norris and two Ryknields. Two Leylands were soon added. An earlier Critchley-Norris was a charabanc bought by the Burnley Motor Pleasure Co of Burnley in 1906; it ran for a number of years.

Crompton

Electrical company Crompton was involved with two battery-electric buses. One, in 1909, was on a chassis built by Motor Omnibus Construction at Walthamstow for trials with the LGOC. It had a pair of Crompton electric motors and a motor generator. Two years later a further Crompton battery-electric double-decker featured regenerative braking and an 'electric valve' which limited the current that could be taken from the batteries. The latter is thought to be the last battery-electric double-decker built.

Crossley

Crossley Brothers of Gorton, Manchester, had been founded in 1866, and made gas and oil engines for marine and other purposes. The company added car manufacture in 1904 and had its first associations with the bus industry in 1905 when the Lancashire Steam Motor Co (later to become Leyland Motors) bought its engines for double-deckers ordered by the London Suburban Omnibus Co. Leyland was still developing its own petrol engine.

Right:
The maker had a long association with Manchester Corporation, greatly aided by the council's policy of supporting (very) local industry. This is one of the first Mancunians, introduced in 1933; the chassis design had been improved and altered from the earlier Condor partly to meet Manchester's specification. *Author's Collection*

The car business was later transferred to a new company, Crossley Motors, and in 1913 it began supplying one of its models, the 20/25hp, to the Royal Flying Corps as a staff car and as an RFC tender. Thousands were manufactured and after the war many found their way to the civilian market and were rebodied as charabancs or buses, mainly for small operators (often ex-servicemen) just setting up in business. Some were remarkably longlived; four were still being run by Filkins and Ainsworth of Harefield on routes to Uxbridge and Rickmansworth when that company was compulsorily acquired by the LPTB in 1933.

Crossley resumed car building after the war, and involved itself in various other enterprises including an aircraft-building company and the joint venture company, Willys Overland Crossley, which assembled Willys cars and Willys and Manchester trucks. However, the company got into a poor financial state,

partly through dabbling in too many fields and partly because of its endemic habit of redesigning, improving (it hoped) and generally changing everything it made. This increased costs and often reduced reliability — hardly what was intended.

However, in 1928 the bus building business seemed to be doing well, so Crossley launched into this as well. By 1939 it could claim to have some 900 buses in service with 23 different municipalities. These, and a handful of independents, were the only purchasers, unfortunately. Luckily, Manchester Corporation had a policy of firm support for local industry, and not infrequently overrode the recommendations of its transport manager and the transport committee, which meant that 646 of the 900 were in the Manchester fleet. In all Manchester bought over 800 Crossleys; the next biggest was Rochdale with 80, while the corporations of Ashton-under-Lyne and Stockport were other local users.

Crossley's first purpose-built bus was the Eagle forward-control single-decker which was fitted with the 5.3 litre four-cylinder engine and was in production until 1931. The chassis was also offered from 1929 with a six-cylinder 6.8 litre engine, first as the Arrow (until Dennis, which was already using the name, objected), then as the Six and later as the Alpha. A double-deck version appeared in 1930. Initially also called the Six, it was later known as the Condor. The same year saw three Condors built with Gardner 6L2 oil engines, one for Leeds Corporation entering service in September to become the UK's first diesel double-decker.

Crossley was also developing its own diesel engine, completing the first in December 1930 to be able to win fame as the first British maker to offer a complete diesel-engine bus — Crossley also built the body. Oil engines soon gained acceptance and few further petrol Crossleys were built. Engine improvements followed in 1933, though the chassis was strangely dated in other ways, with its central accelerator pedal and right-hand gate gearchange. But the Ricardo-designed cylinder head was a decided step for the better.

A new double-deck model for 1934 was the Mancunian, appropriately named as it was developed mainly to meet a Manchester Corporation specification. The gearbox was mounted directly behind the engine. Similar changes were made to the Alpha single-decker, but batches for Manchester in 1937 and Sunderland Corporation in 1939 were the only ones made and carried the Mancunian name. Engine design changed again, with the production of a short stroke model of slightly lower output; the main aim was to try and improve bearing and crankshaft life which was (and continued to be) well below that of rival makes.

Various gearbox options were offered at times. Crossley's interest in this subject was to come to fruition after World War 2 as another technical chal-

Above:
One of the few buyers of Crossleys in the late 1930s other than Manchester, was Maidstone Corporation. This 1940 example also carried a Crossley body and was fitted with a Crossley diesel engine. *Author's Collection*

lenge not to be missed! A four-speed sliding mesh gearbox had been standard since 1928, but Bury Corporation had a pre-selector in a petrol-engined Condor in 1931 and Barrow-in-Furness Corporation took a batch of diesel-engined Condors with pre-selectors in 1932. Northampton Corporation, one of Crossley's few non-local customers (others were Aberdeen, Maidstone and Portsmouth corporations) standardised on pre-selectors. A constant-mesh gearbox was offered from the mid-1930s, while Manchester had a few Mancunians with synchromesh gearboxes. In 1936 both Manchester and Rochdale tried a bus with Freeborn four-speed semi-automatic gearbox. All this variety and experimentation might have been fine for a company building hundreds of buses every year, but when total production barely reached four figures over 12 years it must have imposed a tremendous financial burden.

There was no wartime production of Crossleys, but Manchester was able to take delivery of 70 Gardner 5LW engines in 1943 that had been intended for Daimler chassis it had on order. The Daimler chassis (and much of the factory) had been destroyed in the Blitz, but Manchester fitted the engines to Mancunians in its fleet, making them the most reliable Crossleys it ran.

CWS Bell

Retail co-operative societies used to be big users of vehicles, mainly for deliveries, but some also ran charabancs and coaches, while a select few even operated bus services. The Co-operative Wholesale Society began assembling chassis in Manchester in 1919 using patterns and designs bought from Bell Brothers. Initially 3/4, 1 and 1 1/2 ton chassis were produced, all using the same 2.5 litre engine. A Dorman-engined 1 1/2-2 ton chassis with overhead worm drive was added in 1922; some were bodied as charabancs. Five years later a larger model was added; most were bodied as 20-seat PSVs. Three years later all production ceased.

Daimler

Daimler was one of the earliest British manufacturers, but unlike most builders of PSV chassis did not make trucks (except during World War 1); its other products were cars. The name came from Gottlieb Daimler, the German from whom the company bought the British patent rights. Its early history was complicated until the formation of Daimler Motor Co (1904). Daimler had built a petrol-electric double-decker in 1908, and its subsidiary, the Gearless Motor Omnibus, produced two years later a remarkable integral double-decker — the KPL. This had an engine on each side, electric transmission, accumulators that could provide extra power, and worm drive. It was probably too complicated to be practical, and also attracted accusations of patent infringements.

In 1911 Frank Searle, of LGOC 'B'-type design fame, joined Daimler and designed a more conventional bus, the 'CC'-type, with sleeve-valve Daimler engine (as used in its cars) and an ordinary gearbox. Many were bought by British Automobile Traction, a subsidiary of the British Electric Traction Group, which had realised the limitations of the tram and was setting up bus companies.

One BET subsidiary was Metropolitan Electric Tramways, which formed the Tramways (MET) Omnibus Co in 1912. Searle sold it 100 Daimlers, agreeing to maintain them at 3 1/2d (1.5p) a mile for three years. He then revealed this to A. H. Stanley of the Underground Group, whose LGOC bus and tube activities surrounded MET's area, and won a counter-order for 250 Daimlers. Searle then went back to MET, who outbid Stanley by agreeing to buy 350, but at a lower maintenance cost of 3d a mile. At the time it was the largest bus order ever placed.

However, Searle had not endeared himself to either side, and Stanley (later to become Lord Ashfield) negotiated with Daimler. The MET order was cut back to 226, and 124 AEC 'B'-types were added. Compensation for Daimler came by making it the sole agent for outside sales of AEC. From then on, there was considerable co-operation between the two, culminating in the unsuccessful ADC merger in the mid-1920s. Daimler also sold large numbers of its own buses up to World War 1, and was probably the largest builder after AEC.

During the war the 'Y'-type replaced the similar 'CC', and was built in quantity mainly for the military. Subsequently, the company was slow to develop new models, the double-deck 'CK' and the single-deck 'CL' and 'CM'-types differing in minor detail only from wartime models. All were still normal control although Daimler did pioneer pneumatic tyres on single-deckers, particularly charabancs.

When production under its own name restarted after the dissolution of AEC, designer Lawrence Pomeroy's first model was the CF6. This had a 5.7 litre six-cylinder engine and a radiator with the distinctive fluted top. The following year — 1930 — saw the arrival of the CG6, a much more modern chassis with wider track and lower frame. Later the same year came the CH6, which combined two separate inventions — the fluid coupling and the pre-selective epicyclic gearbox. But if the fluid transmission was modern, the sleeve-valve engine with its high consumption of lubricating oil was not.

Left:
The huge MET order helped establish Daimler as a major builder, supplying many fleets. Manchester Corporation bought eight 'CCs' in 1913 and 1914, lost them to the military, but managed to obtain three 'CCs' in 1915 and five similar 'Ys' in 1916. *Author's Collection*

That was changed in 1932 with the CP6, which had a new poppet-valve 6.6 litre engine.

But with the UK economy stagnant, production was probably little more than one a week. Then, at the 1933 Commercial Vehicle Show, Daimler produced the COG5, a diesel with the Gardner 5LW seven-litre engine. Gardner economy and reliability, coupled with the ease of driving a pre-selector made the model most attractive for urban operation. Also offered was the COG6, with the 8.4 litre, six-cylinder Gardner; and the COA6, with AEC's six-cylinder diesel for which Coventry Corporation was the only (but regular) buyer.

Above:
This was Daimler's 'new silent engine developing 40hp at 1,000rpm as used by the LGOC on the London bus service where it has become famous for its silence ...'. That was Daimler's 1914 claim, and of course its sleeve-valve engine was much quieter. But in London it was fitted only in the MET buses (and an associated fleet) which were under LGOC management, and against the LGOC's 'B'-type AECs the Daimlers were in the minority. *Author's Collection*

Right:
The CP6 model was a much improved vehicle all round, and Daimler had accepted the inevitable and designed a poppet-valve engine. Soon the chassis would gain the diesel engine and become far more popular. But this Cleethorpes Corporation CP6 with Willowbrook body lasted into the postwar years. Cleethorpes later merged with Grimsby Corporation. *Roy Marshall*

Right:
This AEC-engined utility Daimler was one of a batch delivered to Portsmouth Corporation in 1944. All had Duple bodies, and all were fitted with new bodies (by Crossley) in 1955. Body deterioration through the use of poor quality materials was the main problem with utility buses generally. *Ian Allan Library*

Production rose rapidly. Birmingham Corporation alone took 100 chassis before the end of 1934. The model changed little over the years, except for the addition of flexible three-point mountings. There was also a COG5/40 single-decker with shorter bonnet and more upright radiator to allow bodywork for up to 40 seats.

All building ceased abruptly in 1940 after the factory was bombed. Production of diesel-engined chassis had run at about 300 a year over the previous six years. Surprisingly, the Ministry of Supply found Daimler a requisitioned factory, in Wolverhampton, and production got under way in December 1942 with the CWG5, an austerity version of the prewar model. The fluid flywheel and pre-selector gearbox were retained, perhaps because redesign would have taken too long, but no alloys were used and unladen weight was therefore heavier. By the middle of 1943 100 had been built, after which Daimler switched to the CWA6, with AEC engine, of which Daimler had also had previous experience. By mid-1945 some 630 of these had been completed, but another engine was now available — from Daimler itself. The company

had been working on its own design of 8.6 litre six-cylinder engine since about 1936 until the outbreak of war, but a prototype engine and all drawings and test records were lost when the factory was bombed. The first production chassis with the new engine was completed early in 1945, after which AEC and Daimler-engined chassis were built together. It is perhaps surprising that the Ministry of Supply permitted work on the engine to resume, and even more remarkable that Daimler was able to 'recreate' its engine at such a time. Presumably AEC and Gardner were at full capacity, and the Ministry saw that something had to be done.

Darracq-Serpollet

The Metropolitan Steam Omnibus Co, formed in 1907, built up in five years a fleet of over 50 Darracq-Serpollet steam buses — the second largest steam bus fleet in London. And yet, before the end of 1912, all had gone, to be replaced by 'B'-type petrol buses under an agreement with the LGOC. Failure followed the bankruptcy of Darracq-Serpollet, of which the operator was a subsidiary. The French company Darracq had formed Darracq-Serpollet to make steam vehicles using Serpollet's design, including the flash boiler. It had formed the Metropolitan company because it realised that this was the only way to sell steam buses; Clarkson with his buses came to the same conclusion a couple of years later. Three of the Darracq-Serpollets survived to run on the Isle of Wight until about 1923.

Below:
A. H. Creeth & Sons built up a fleet of seven steam buses of various makes by the early 1920s for their Ryde, Seaview & District Motor Services business on the Isle of Wight. This was one of three Darracq-Serpollet steam buses that had been new to the Metropolitan Steam Omnibus Co in London and was photographed in 1915. *Author's Collection*

De Dion-Bouton

'Despite its multiplicity of parts, the De Dion was among the most efficient and economical of the older type of bus before the 'B'.' according to W. J. Iden, one-time chief engineer of the LGOC. Its flitched wooden chassis frame was copied on the 'B'-type. Both London General and Vanguard ran de Dions in London, their combined fleets totalling 160 of this make. The manufacturer had a long history. It began in 1884 and finally faded away after World War 2. Double-deckers built for the French market from 1905 had a cab-over-engine layout and, of course, the De Dion axle. There were other, later, examples of De Dion in the UK and in 1928 Highland Motorways put a long-wheelbase normal control example into service. It made three runs a week in each direction between Glasgow and Inverness. It had an unusual single-deck coach body by Strachan & Brown with raised 'observation' section above the rear axle.

Delahaye

One of the oldest and longest-established French manufacturers was Delahaye, which made its first car in 1894 and added commercial vehicles to its range before 1900. Its real entry into the PSV market came in 1923 with a modest-sized vehicle fitted with pneumatic tyres, four-wheel brakes and — unusually — worm-driven back axle. A few were sold in the UK and Midland Bus Services, later to be a constituent of Western SMT, bought two in 1924. They had 20-seat bodies and survived until 1932.

Dennis

In the 1990s Dennis is virtually the only surviving British-owned bus builder, and in its long life the company has seen remarkable ups and downs. It was enormously successful in the late 1920s and early 1930s, and then slowly lost out again with a mix of

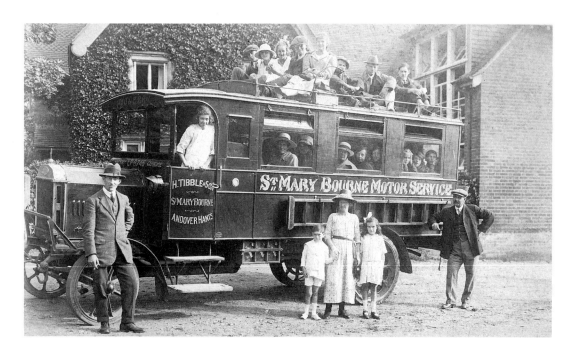

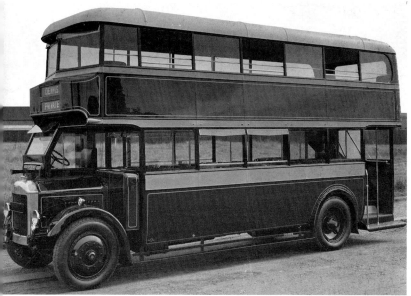

Above:
A bus body has been mounted on this War Department-type Dennis chassis. It was operated by the St Mary Bourne Motor Service, based near Andover. Photographed in 1919, it has the proprietor of the business, Mr H. Tibble, leaning on the ladder which could be unhooked to give access to the roof. The driver stands by the front wheel. *Author's Collection*

Left:
The first purpose-built double-decker was the Dennis 'H'. This example with Hall Lewis body was a show exhibit for 1928. It looks relatively smart and modern, apart from the clumsy front, but it still had a cone clutch and the upper-deck seating was longitudinal. *Ian Allan Library*

good and disappointing designs. It vacillated with its own and proprietary diesel engines long after the likes of AEC, Daimler and Leyland had settled for reliable products, and its Lance double-deckers of the mid to late 1930s suffered from chassis frame weaknesses, radiator problems and various other faults.

Despite these problems, Dennis's sales and technical successes were considerable. In the early years of the motorbus it perfected a quiet and satisfactory shaft-drive back axle; it was the first to introduce four-wheel brakes to a London bus; and it had some

of the first London buses on pneumatic tyres. Its 'E' and later 'EV'-type single-deckers sold very well in the late 1920s, as did their successor, the Lancet. But the multiplicity of smaller models of the 1930s — the Aces, Maces, Arrow Minors and Pikes — were up against enormous competition from Leyland's Cub downwards to mass-produced Bedfords, Dodges, Commers and others. Total sales of the Mace, which was a forward-control Ace, were well under 100 in four years.

The Dennis story began before 1900, with bicycles,

Right:
This unusual style of coach body was offered by Dennis on its latest Lancet chassis in 1932. It was a fully-equipped 32-seater complete with interior luggage racks. Total cost of the complete vehicle was £1,050. *Ian Allan Library*

Below right:
The first Dennis Aces and Maces joined the fleets of the Western National Omnibus Co and the Southern National Omnibus Co in 1934. This is the larger model, the Mace, with 26 coat body by Eastern Counties. It is seen negotiating the narrow streets of Mousehole, on the service to Penzance. *Author's Collection*

Below:
Aldershot & District Traction, with headquarters not many miles from the Dennis works, was the make's best customer for many years. This Lance double-decker has a Gardner 5LW engine and a later East Lancs body. It lasted with Aldershot & District until the late 1950s. *Author*

and quickly moved on through motorised tricycles and larger cars to commercial vehicles by 1904. The first bus was produced the following year, but passenger-carrying vehicles were based on goods chassis until 1925. A very early user of Dennis was Provincial Tramways of Grimsby with its first 30hp double-decker in 1906. The most enduring of customers was the local company, Aldershot & District Traction Co, which began buying the type before 1914. Dennis built more of its own components than many rivals, but from 1909 fitted White and Poppe petrol engines, later buying the company and still later moving the production and staff to an extended Dennis factory in Guildford.

After World War 1 Dennis offered its own bodywork for its products. A four-ton chassis announced in 1921 was said to be ideal for double-deck bodywork. A 1924 40/50hp chassis for Nottingham had a Short Bros 50-seat covered-top body — an early example of a closed-top double-decker. The first PSV specifically designed as such was the 'E'-type, with dropped frame and forward-control layout. It had a four-cylinder engine, but later a six was an option. The companion 'F'-type, with dropped frame but normal control, was popular with coach operators. Forward-control double-deckers first appeared with the 'H'-type of 1927.

A model with a name successfully revived in recent years is the Dart. It first appeared in 1930 as a normal-control chassis with six-cylinder engine and servo-brakes. Popular with independent operators, it also became the standard small bus with the LGOC. The 1934 Ace was a compact and manoeuvrable single-decker with the engine over and forward of the front axle. It became widely used by Tilling companies such as West Yorkshire Road Car Co, Western and Southern National, and Southern Vectis. This was no doubt partly because neither Bristol nor TSM offered vehicles of this size.

Dennis-Stevens

Towards the end of World War 1 a petrol-electric chassis known as the Dennis-Stevens was introduced. Like the better-known Tilling-Stevens it incorporated the designs of W. A. Stevens, with the vehicle's petrol engine (a 40hp Dennis) being used to drive an electric motor. Radiators were badged just 'Stevens' and were larger than usual. A water pump was also fitted.

Below:
Dodge's 20-seater was of normal-control layout, but the 26-seater introduced later was of semi-forward-control. This Harrington-bodied example, dating from 1938, was built for Valliant Direct Coaches and was unusual in managing to accommodate 29 seats.
Author's Collection

Early chassis were bodied as searchlights or mobile workshops, but later ones carried bus bodies. Tram operator Cardiff Corporation bought six single-deckers as its first buses in 1920, adding six double-deckers in 1922. Ease of driving was no doubt the reason for the purchases. The Cardiff buses lasted until 1930-31, but two were then rebodied as tower wagons and these ran until 1951.

Diamond T

Trucks built by the North American maker Diamond T were sold in the UK for a number of years in the 1930s and in 1937 a normal-control chassis was also offered for PSV use with up to 25 seats.

Dodge (Britain)

American-built Dodge chassis had been imported into the UK since the early 1920s and assembled here since 1927. Dodge Bros (Britain) had been formed when imports had built up to a considerable volume and, in 1933 at Kew, Surrey, the company started to produce its own range, while continuing to use US engines and gearboxes. A 20-seat bus was first listed in 1934, with six-cylinder 23hp petrol engine, hydraulic brakes and spiral bevel rear axle. In 1937 a 26-seat model was added, and from 1938 this was the only PSV produced.

Dodge (US)

A strange purchase by Southend Corporation in 1945 was of eight North American-built normal-control Dodges, complete with bodies. They had been used in the UK by the Royal Canadian Air Force. Southend undertook rebuilding, but it was a long process and it

took until 1948 for the first to be completed and in the end only four ran as PSVs. They were rather longer than most normal-control buses in the UK and seated 28 when rebuilt.

Ducommun

This German maker built commercial vehicles with shaft drive for about three years and a number were operated in London by the Rapid Road Transport Co (fleetname Rapide) in London for a few months during 1906 until the company went out of business. The buses were sold for further use at Hastings but lasted less than a year there before that operator also went into liquidation.

Durham-Churchill and Hallamshire

The Sheffield company of Durham, Churchill & Co built Hallamshire cars and Churchills or Durham-Churchills. It completed at least one Hallamshire charabanc, with 20hp engine, and demonstrated it by running with a full load of passengers from Sheffield to Doncaster Races and return on four consecutive days in 1905. The charabanc left on its 20-mile run well after the horse-drawn conveyances, and arrived well before them.

The same year saw the start of production of Churchills or Durham-Churchills, which petered out some 20 years later, with a gap in the war years. Early models had Aster 24 or 30hp engines.

The best-known vehicle must be the roofed charabanc bought by the Caledonian Railway. First operated on a trial basis in 1906, it was found satisfactory and purchased. After two years' work alongside a Darracq-Serpollet steam bus, the route was discontinued as uneconomic. The Durham-Churchill was then fitted with flanged wheels and, still with its open-sided body and tiered seats, ran as a rail motor between Connel Ferry and Benderloch.

At the other end of the British Isles, newly-formed Southdown Motor Services ran four Durham-Churchill charabancs on stage services in 1915 when it was very short of vehicles; they had been bought new the previous year by one of Southdown's constituents, London & South Coast Haulage Co.

Durkopp

German maker Durkopp built bus chassis from about 1902 until the late 1920s, but probably only the early models were sold in the UK. An early operator was the North Eastern Railway, which built up a fleet of 15 or more, while across the border the Glasgow & South Western Railway and the Great North of Scotland Railway both operated some. The Great Western Railway bought some, but cancelled a second order, apparently finding problems with the crankshafts and chassis frames. London horsebus proprietor Patrick Hearn had a few, whilst others ran briefly at Hastings before their operator went bankrupt.

Below:
The North Eastern Railway was a pioneer bus operator, and an early user of Durkopp chassis. The railway often built its own bodies, as on this chassis, which was one of five delivered in 1905. This, and two others, had charabanc bodies, while the remaining two had single-deck bus bodies. *Author's Collection*

Economist

Badge engineering is nothing new. Just before World War 1 Clayton & Co (Huddersfield) made Karrier Cars charabanc chassis with different radiator shells, badged 'Economist', for sale by Stagg & Robson of Selby, Yorkshire.

Edison

Several towns tried one or more Edison battery-electric buses. The earliest was Southend. The corporation bought just one, based on a US-built GMC chassis with Edison electric motors and Brush body. It ran from 1914 until 1916. The municipalities of Derby, Lancaster, South Shields, West Bromwich and York, along with Loughborough Road Car, all ran Edisons. Probably the best known were at Lancaster, which eventually had five. A booster station or recharging point was usually provided at the town centre termini. The Edisons at West Bromwich replaced four Albions that were less than a month old and which had been

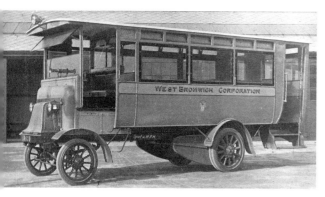

commandeered by the Army. The Edisons also inherited the Albions' bodies.

Electrobus

The London Electrobus Co ran battery-powered buses in London from 1907 to 1910 and may have demonstrated vehicles earlier. The buses were assembled by the Electric Vehicle Co, West Norwood, London, and included French components. Like other pioneering operations, the buses were not profitable and all 12 were subsequently bought by the Brighton, Hove & Preston United Omnibus Co, which had also bought three new Electrobuses the previous year. It dismantled four of the ex-London buses as spares for the rest and also bought a fourth new vehicle. The last one survived until 1917.

Enfield

Originally connected with the Royal Enfield Co (of cycle and motorcycle fame), this maker built a few commercial vehicles up to about 1915. Originally based in Redditch, it later moved to Birmingham, and subsequently was acquired by Alldays & Onions. A 35hp Enfield with substantial 26-seat bus body was put into service during 1914 by the Mid Cheshire Motor Bus Co and ran for 10 years, being scrapped after North Western Road Car bought Mid Cheshire.

Fageol

American truck maker Fageol, of Oakland, California, soon discovered that the western states of the USA needed more powerful vehicles to cope with the long hills and other arduous conditions encountered there. The Fageol brothers, Frank R. and William B., collaborated with Col E. W. Hall of Hall-Scott Motor Car Co to produce their Safety Bus in 1921. Quickly renamed Safety Coach, it was of normal-control layout, but with a very low chassis frame, powerful four-cylinder Hall-Scott engine and enclosed body-

Above left:
This is one of West Bromwich Corporation's four Edisons; it was fitted with registration number and body from an Albion that had been commandeered by the Army. The Edisons cost £890 each plus £50 for adapting and fitting the bodies, which were converted to rear entrance. The chassis proved notoriously unreliable. *Ian Allan Library*

Left:
This was London's prototype Electrobus, with chassis built by Improved Electric Traction; it was fitted with BTH motors and a body by T. H. Lewis of Chalk Farm, London. In 1907-08 it was followed by a production batch of 20, with different chassis and body builders. *Author's Collection*

Right:
Fageols were rare in Europe, but well-known Irish operator H. M. S. Catherwood ran one. Most of the operator's fleet was supplied by Leyland. *Geoff Lumb Collection*

work seating 22, with a separate door to each row of seats. A larger model, with gangwayed body seating 29 and with a 100hp six-cylinder Hall-Scott engine, soon followed. The growing production soon had to be moved to a separate plant in Kent, Ohio.

More than 250 were built in 1923 and almost double that in 1924. The American Car & Foundry Co bought the Ohio bus factory and moved production to Detroit in 1926, bringing the Fageol brothers with it. New models were added with those after 1928 going under the 'ACF' name. But bus production also continued in a modest way at the original Oakland factory, which had not been taken over by ACF. Later, ACF was unenthusiastic about a new design of high capacity city bus with two engines, so the Fageol brothers left and formed a new company, Twin Coach Co.

A number of Safety Coaches were imported into the UK, but the Metropolitan Police refused to licence any of these low single-deckers because they had four-wheel brakes and pneumatic tyres.

Fargo

Some American Dodges were badged as 'Fargo', but in addition for a time Dodge built some Fargo-badged chassis that were not built also as Dodge. The Fargo Freighter was a one-ton truck that was also offered in the UK up to 1930 as a 14-seat PSV.

Just to confuse matters further, though strictly outside the scope of this book, some British-built Dodge chassis in the 1930s were exported as Fargos.

Federal

Detroit, Michigan, was the home of the Federal Motor Truck Co, one of the more successful assemblers of commercial vehicles; every component was bought in. Some had been sold in the UK in 1914 but the make faded from the UK scene in the mid-1920s, only to reappear in 1929 with four different normal-control models. These seated between 20 and 32 and were said to have been imported from Canada; they were not available after 1930.

Federal did not produce purpose-built PSV chassis until the early 1920s, when 18 and 25-seaters were offered with six-cylinder Willys-Knight engines. Later there was a choice of Waukesha four-cylinder or Continental six-cylinder engines.

Fiat

Italian Fiat chassis were sold in the UK at various times. Some early ones were bought by pioneer bus operator Bristol Tramways, but they were not satisfactory; in 1910 Bristol won substantial damages against the supplier for vehicles which had not met the company's specification. The buses apparently found Bristol's hills too much. The North Eastern Railway, however, seemed happier, buying 18 with 29 or 34-seat charabanc bodies between 1907 and 1910.

Some surplus World War 1 Fiats were reconditioned in the UK after being brought back from conti-

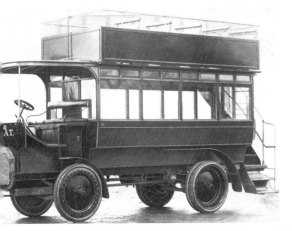

Left:
A few Fiats were imported in the very early days. This 1905 24hp double-decker was described at the time as having 'forward drive' — a reference to the driver's position. *Author's Collection*

Left:
Although the floor height is not particularly low for what would today be termed a small bus, the two-step entrance and folding door on this Fiat are quite neat. Vehicles of this size enjoyed a — legal — speed advantage in the 1920s; if weighing under two tons they could run at 20mph, while larger buses were limited to 12mph. *Arthur Ingram Collection*

Below left:
The opposite extreme to the small wagonettes tried by some pioneer operators was this American-built Fischer battery-electric imported by the LGOC. It was too heavy and too wide ever to enter public service. *Author's Collection*

Below:
Foden's first Bandmaster chassis was bodied for the company's brass band. It had the four-cylinder Gardner LW engine. The passengers in this picture are unlikely members of the band. *Ian Allan Library*

nental battlefields by one E. B. Horne, better remembered for similarly acquired Garfords and for setting up the Gilford company.

Other Fiats were imported new in the 1920s. Biggest buyer was probably Scottish Motor Traction Co, which bought over 80 between 1921 and 1926. All were 14-seaters, mainly charabancs, but also some buses. All had been disposed of by the end of 1929.

Fischer

An American Fischer petrol-electric bus was the first motorbus bought by the LGOC. Ordered in June 1902, it was not delivered until spring 1903 and cost £450. Its petrol engine drove a generator which in turn fed two electric motors, one on each rear wheel. It was very heavy and also exceeded the permitted width of 6ft 6in (1.98m), but ran trials, fully laden, on

two nights and once during the daytime. In October 1903 the LGOC asked the suppliers to take it back and refund the price.

Foden

Foden persevered longer than most with steam-powered goods vehicles, but the early 1930s saw the company introduce diesels. Strangely, the first PSV chassis, built in 1933 and named the Bandmaster, was for carrying the famous Foden brass band. Of forward-control layout, it had the Gardner 4LW engine to the nearside of the driver but angled so that the transmission line ran diagonally across the chassis to an offset and offside housing for the worm-driven rear axle.

The Olympia Show that year saw a Burlingham-bodied Bandmaster for Green Bus Service. Foden built a small number of single-deckers with the larger Gardner 6LW, and also three double-deckers.

Ford and Fordson

Almost everybody has heard of the Ford 'T', arguably the most successful car and light commercial vehicle ever built. It and the related one-ton 'TT' were identical whether built in the US factory or in the British plant established in Trafford Park, Manchester, in 1911. The two-speed epicyclic gearbox was a particular asset in the days when few possessed driving skills or mechanical aptitude! Fords formed the basis of many — probably the majority — of the fleets of the rural operators who began in the years after World

Above:
This country carrier's Ford 'T' is at the opposite end of the spectrum to the Stockton example, but its value to inhabitants of a rural area would have been considerable. *Geoff Lumb Collection*

War 1. Not only was the chassis cheap to buy and relatively reliable, but spares were widely available. The 'TT' was a lengthened 'T', but several companies offered kits to lengthen (or further lengthen) chassis, and auxiliary gearboxes were also available from some. Not all Fords were on rural routes; a number of operators used them on short urban services.

UK Ford production later moved to Dagenham and the 'AA' model replaced the 'T'. As a PSV the 'AA' was advertised as seating up to 14, whereas its 'BB' successor of 1933 could accommodate up to 20. An unusual feature was the V8 petrol engine, which was for a time offered only in PSV models and not in the basic lorries. Ford commercials were renamed Fordsons from 1933.

Among operators of the 'BB' was David Lawson, later part of the Alexander bus empire in Scotland, which bought four with 14-seat bus bodies in 1935. Another buyer that year was the Redbourn Group, which controlled a number of operators in the Thanet area of Kent. It also had four, with Duple 20-seat coach bodies. East Kent took over the company later that year and soon disposed of the Fords. Two of them, however, survived almost 20 years more with subsequent owners.

Frick

Leeds-based Dougill's Engineering built commercial vehicles under the 'Frick' name from 1904 until the company went into receivership in 1907. One, fitted with a single-deck bus body, was shown at the 1906 Agricultural Hall Show held at Islington, London. It was a 22-seater with three-cylinder 7.2 litre engine.

Another bus was said to have been exported to Egypt. A feature of the vehicles was the unusual drive, via discs, friction wheels and finally two-step chain gearing. Speed variations were obtained by rotating a wheel beneath the steering wheel.

FS Petrol Electric Equipment Co

Percy Frost Smith had been chief engineer of Thomas Tilling and involved in the design of the first petrol-electrics. Subsequently, as joint managing director of Tilling-Stevens, he designed its postwar petrol-electrics. In 1920 he resigned, set up as a consulting engineer, and designed the FS Petrol Electric. This is best described as an improved version of the Tilling-Stevens. Initially, six were assembled at Highbury, North London, using bought-in components for many parts, including Dennis units, White & Poppe petrol engines (as used by Dennis) and Kirkstall back axles.

Frost Smith put the six to work in London, but never managed to sell (or build) any more. Surprisingly, they were not very reliable, either. Before the end of 1924 the company, by now the FS Petrol Electric Omnibus Co, was bankrupt and wound up. Frost Smith died suddenly, less than a month later after a day's illness.

Garford

One of several US makes to be found in the UK after World War 1, Garfords were, in a sense, the forerunners of Gilford. After the war E. B. Horne had set up in London selling former Garford military chassis, most of which were recovered from continental battlefields. He himself often brought the chassis back to the Holloway, London, workshops where the chassis were stripped down and reconditioned and the engines overhauled. Some Fiats and other makes were also handled, but of over 500 vehicles dealt with in this way most were Garfords. By 1925 E. B. Horne and his partner had decided to go one step further and build new chassis of their own design for PSV use — Gilfords.

Garner

Top salesman Henry Garner began selling US-built trucks under his name in World War 1. Assembly in Birmingham with UK-sourced components ultimately

followed. The most interesting PSV was the first, the Garner Patent Busvan of 1921. A complete vehicle, it was aimed at country carriers. It could carry up to 20 passengers or up to $1\frac{3}{4}$ tons (1,780kg) of goods, or a combination. Seats faced inwards (and could be folded up alongside the sides) and there was an entrance alongside the driver. At the back were twin hinged doors for loading freight.

Four years later came a proper PSV, of normal-control layout, with a low frame and four-wheel brakes. A 1928 announcement was of a 'high-speed passenger chassis' for 20-seat bus or coach bodywork. Surprisingly, it had a straight chassis frame; perhaps the company read the market correctly in assuming that small, competing operators wanted something fast and with a good engine.

Above:
Percy Frost Smith ran a total of six of his own design of petrol-electrics between 1922 and 1924 in London. However, the venture failed and he did not manage to sell any of his design to other operators. *Author's Collection*

Right:
The Garner Progressor chassis was designed as a de luxe model for 20-seat bodywork. It came complete with outriggers already fitted and had an Austin 20 engine. *Author's Collection*

In 1933 the Precursor 20-seater and Progressor were introduced. The latter was a de luxe version of the former with a strange mix of extras including chassis outriggers (ready for body attachment) and front bumper — plus a tyre pump.

However, PSV production, such as it was, faded. The company became controlled by Sentinel, later went bankrupt, and then was rescued by some ex-Chrysler employees. But no more PSVs were built.

Germain

Germain was a Belgian builder of railway equipment which, for a brief period, also constructed cars and commercial vehicles. Among the latter was a 16/20hp

double-decker with the driver seated on top of the engine and with an upright steering column. The London Road Car Co took delivery of one in 1904, and two or three years later added a further 10. These were of a more conventional normal-control layout. They were apparently sufficiently troublesome to have to be returned to Belgium for rectification work.

Gilford

If the Gilford story had taken place in the 1980s it would have made compulsive viewing on a television programme about industry and business. But this was the 1920s and 1930s, when failure of vehicle makers was no novelty. However, what made the Gilford

story different was the dramatic swing in fortune; it became a public company in 1929 and proceeded to pay a first-year dividend of a remarkable 33$\frac{1}{3}$%, but two years later made a loss, subsequently sliding into bankruptcy in 1935.

The sad end to a company whose products were, generally, good can be attributed to four causes. It had sold mainly to independent operators, and they were a declining breed with the advent of proper licensing controls and takeovers by larger companies. It lost money when those small operators who survived got into financial difficulties and then defaulted on their hire purchase repayments. It had difficulty in keeping up with the continuing stream of design improvements produced by makers such as AEC and Leyland that were benefiting from large orders and the resulting economies of scale. Finally, and unique to Gilford, was the vast amount of money and effort it poured into a project to build and sell a revolutionary low-height, low-floor, front-wheel drive double-decker with opposed piston engine from Junkers.

Gilford had come into being in 1925 when E. B. Horne and V. O. Skinner decided to build their own chassis. Until then they had successfully reconditioned ex-World War 1 American Garfords (and also some Fiats). The first few chassis produced were straight-framed conventional models, with four-cylinder American-designed engines. But following quickly on the heels of AEC's 'NS' and the Maudslay, Gilford produced a drop-frame chassis with American Buda engine. This was soon followed by a similar chassis with a six-cylinder engine. This Low Line Coach (later reclassified LL) was so successful that by the end of 1927 the firm had had to move to larger premises at High Wycombe. A year later came the first forward-control chassis, the version with 16ft 6in (5m) wheelbase and 36hp American Lycoming engine — the 1660T — being a best-seller. The engine gave high torque at low speeds, Gilford saying there was no comparable UK engine.

Worthy of mention for 1928 was the following of a

popular trend towards six-wheelers, Gilford's 6WOT having the usual hydraulic-assisted brakes, on all six wheels, and a large six-cylinder American Wisconsin engine. A new smaller model for 1929 was the CP6, a low-loading chassis for up to 20 seats, or for use as a lorry. Gilford, for most of its life, reversed the usual trend, primarily making PSVs but also having some success with goods vehicles, particularly for export.

Gilford exhibited in its own right at a UK show for the first time at Olympia in 1929, displaying a new version of its successful single-deck models. The vehicles gained distinctive Gruss air springs at the front, and were offered in normal or forward-control layout. A forward-control double-decker was also available. All three had Lycoming six-cylinder side-valve engines, of slightly larger capacity than before. However, it was the single-deckers that sold. East London independent Hillmans of Romford (later compulsorily taken over by the LPTB) placed a large order and numerous other operators bought in ones and twos.

A replacement for the CP6 20-seater came in 1931. Known as the AS6, it dispensed with the Gruss air springs, had a longer wheelbase and numerous design changes. It was said to be the most reliable of all Gilfords. The other model change produced the most unreliable: it was the option of a more powerful engine, a Meadows, in the full-sized single-decker. Later the standard engine, the US Lycoming, was replaced by one built under licence by Coventry Climax, no doubt because of the punitive import duties.

Gilford was the major talking point of the 1931 Olympia Show with its revolutionary double-decker, plus a single-deck version. Enormous and talented design effort had been put into the project, but neither ever found a buyer.

A new model for the following year's Scottish Show was the Zeus, a conventional double-decker with Vulcan Juno engine. It was followed by a single-deck version, the Hera, which luckily was much more successful. Neither had the Gruss air springs at the front, but they did have long leaf springs. Another Zeus and Hera appeared at the 1933 Olympia Show, both fitted with Tangye diesel engines. Both were one-offs; Gilford never sold any more double-deckers despite grand talk of the defeat of the Titans (Leyland) and good press reviews. Continuing economic problems meant Gilfords were no longer cheaper than, say, Leylands. At the end of 1933 Gilford announced it was selling its High Wycombe factory (with the plant's conveyor-belt chassis production facility) and moving to smaller premises on London's North Circular Road. One of the last jobs at High Wycombe was the cutting-up of the revolutionary (and unsaleable) front-wheel drive buses.

One success in 1933 was the winning of orders from W. Alexander and Western SMT for, respectively, 21 and 20 Hera chassis for use on their long-distance coach services. Unusually all 41 were fitted with reconditioned petrol engines supplied by the operators, and Meadows gearboxes and clutches. The engines had come from Leyland chassis which the two operators were fitting with new Leyland diesel engines. The chassis were built in 1934 and accounted for about 70% of that year's total production. By 1935 production was down to about one chassis a week, usually a Hera. However, Gilford persevered, introducing a lightweight model, the PF166 with four-cylinder Perkins diesel engine. Three were sold with full-front Park Royal bodies. A final fling, for the

Below:
The one and only Gilfords (HSG) chassis with its AEC engine and gas producer plant was bodied by Cowieson and bought by Highland Transport of Inverness. The plant was housed in a compartment in the rear offside of the body. *Author's Collection*

1936 London Show, was probably intended to replace the Hera. It was light and had a new design of Coventry Climax petrol engine; a diesel with four-cylinder Gardner unit was also listed but probably not built. However, not long after the show closed its doors, a receiver was appointed and Gilford was subsequently wound-up.

Gilfords (HSG)

High Speed Gas (GB) was a company formed in 1927 to experiment with producer gas as a fuel for commercial vehicles. In 1936 the company acquired the Park Royal premises of Gilford, which was in receivership, and created a new subsidiary — Gilfords (HSG) — to build experimental chassis. Subsequently, it built one bus chassis, based on a 1935 Gilford chassis that, presumably, was lying at Park Royal unsold. It was fitted with a suitably modified AEC engine and an HSG gas producer at the rear (in a separate compartment). Highland Transport of Inverness bought the bus which, apparently, covered some 20,000 miles in the next nine months at an average fuel consumption of 2lb (0.907kg) a mile.

Gloster

The long-established Gloucester Railway Carriage & Wagon had been building bodies since horse-drawn days and then, at a time when export orders had almost vanished, designed and built complete coaches. Most Gloster Gardners were for Red & White Services of Chepstow and the operator had a strong influence on the design. Of the nine built, Red & White took six.

The vehicles had six-cylinder Gardner engines mounted rigidly and five-speed gearboxes mounted flexibly, plus Kirkstall axles. Chassis frames were made by Gloucester, with reinforcing at points of high stress by close-fitting channelling instead of the usual flitch plates. Built in 1933-34, the vehicles were among the first long-distance diesel-engined coaches and could cruise at 50mph. Surprisingly, the bodies did not prove particularly durable — perhaps the rigidly-mounted Gardner engines were bad for them. Red & White fitted new Duple bodies within a few years. A subsequent large order for London Underground trains ended thoughts of building further PSV chassis.

Left:
Red & White was the major operator of Glosters. The body style was neat yet unostentatious, though structurally perhaps suspect. *Arthur Ingram Collection*

Below:
In the late 1920s General Motors was offering both GMC and Chevrolet chassis on the UK market. Pictured on the GM stand at the 1928 motor show is a Grose-bodied 20-seat GMC. *Author's Collection*

GMC

In 1911 the merging of two lorry builders already controlled by General Motors brought about the formation of General Motors Truck Co. This company became General Motors Truck & Coach division in 1925 when American Yellow Coach was merged with it. However, smaller PSVs based on truck chassis were still sold as GMCs. They were usually designed for about 20-seat bodies. A late 1920s Olympia Show saw one stand exhibiting both Chevrolet and GMC buses and coaches.

Gotfredson

One of the least-remembered makes from the 1920s is the Gotfredson, which was built in Canada. It was imported by Bonallack & Sons of London, a company later to make its name as a truck bodybuilder. The chassis were said to be speedy and have excellent hill-climbing abilities. Operators in the Eastern Counties bought a number, but others could be found else-where. For example, the Caledonian Omnibus Co took over a 1924 example from a two-vehicle oper-ator, although it was scrapped in 1928. Western National acquired two from independents taken over in the late 1920s and early 1930s.

Graham Dodge and Graham

Strictly speaking, there was no such make as Graham Dodge, though some US-built chassis imported to the UK undoubtedly ran under that name. Graham Brothers of Indiana assembled truck chassis with Dodge engines from the early 1920s. Dodge itself had an interest in the company and later chassis were built in a Dodge factory. Finally, Dodge took over the company, which became its Graham Bros Division in 1928. A year later the name on the trucks also changed to Dodge. The products were typical North American designs of the period.

Granton

The Scottish Motor Engineering Co, of Granton, Edinburgh, built Granton lorry and bus chassis between 1905 and 1907, no doubt in very small numbers. The 30/40 and 45/50hp engines had four cylinders, a normal speed of 750rpm, and were said to be designed to withstand rough usage. At the 1907 Edinburgh Motor Show the company showed a 30/40hp open-top double-decker seating 36 which was said to have been built generally in accordance with Metropolitan Police Regulations. A similar bus, with a 45/50hp engine, was said to be 'doing good service' on the Edinburgh-Tollcross circular route.

Great Eastern Railway

As a result of the locomotive superintendent of the GER believing that the Milnes-Daimlers the company had bought in 1904 were expensive, 12 double-deckers were built in its own Stratford, east London,

railway workshops in 1904-5. Virtually every part was home-made, but the substantial construction of the vehicles did not ensure reliability.

GNR(I)

Buses built for itself by the Great Northern Railway Co of Ireland at its Dundalk railway works were claimed not to be mere assembly jobs, although they were fitted with Gardner 5LW diesel engines and proprietary axles and gearboxes. The railway claimed it manufactured its own chassis frames, radiators and springs as well as building the bodies. All told, 95 were constructed between 1937 and 1952. They were known as GNR-Gardners and all were forward-control single-deckers.

The first batch had David Brown gearboxes, but later ones were fitted with Leyland units, giving strength to the story that the vehicles were really Gardner-engined Leyland Lions; the GNR(I) had previously bought the Lion in petrol form.

Building its own vehicles saved payment on an import duty of 12¹/₂% imposed on chassis brought in in 'knocked down' form for local assembly. Unusual features of the first batch were the dumb irons, spring brackets and other castings, all of which were of bronze as the GNR(I)'s foundry could not produce steel castings.

Greenwood & Batley

The old-established electrical engineers Greenwood & Batley designed and built a petrol-electric bus chassis in 1907. It had a French Mutel four-cylinder engine driving a generator which powered an electric motor. The motor had two separate armatures each driving a separate gear via driving shafts engaging with the cast steel road wheels.

Guy

Sidney Guy left the then successful Sunbeam Motor Co, where he had been works manager, in 1913 to set up his own company, Guy Motors, the following year. Guy began with small vehicles, notably a 1¹/₂-ton truck chassis with pressed steel frame. During World War 1 the Wolverhampton factory produced armaments not vehicles and after the war there was a brief foray into the car market. Soon models for PSV use included a 30-seat charabanc and a small one-man bus. A landmark in 1924 was production of a drop-frame chassis, as pioneered by AEC only a year previously, though the Guy was of normal-control layout.

Guy, like Karrier, was quick to see the potential for six-wheelers, offering a 60-seater with pneumatic tyres and normal control in 1926. This was before it had even built a two-axle double-decker or a three-axle single-decker. Its six-wheelers were longer lived than Karriers of the same period, but not without problems. Axle and spring location, and the stresses and strains of double drive, were insufficiently understood. A forward-control six-wheel double-decker followed in 1927, the first going to the London Public Omnibus Co. It had met the stringent requirements of Scotland Yard's public carriage office, and further orders for London independents followed. Originally, the six-wheelers had Guy four-cylinder or Daimler-Knight six-cylinder sleeve-valve engines, with Guy producing its own six-cylinder engine in 1927. Guy always had an eye for publicity and around 1930 claimed its products were 'ten years in advance of the times'. Sometimes the publicity was a little short even on genuine fact, but the six-cylinder engine with its inclined side valves did offer some of the advantages of overhead valve engines without the complexity, as was claimed. Improved versions of the six-wheelers

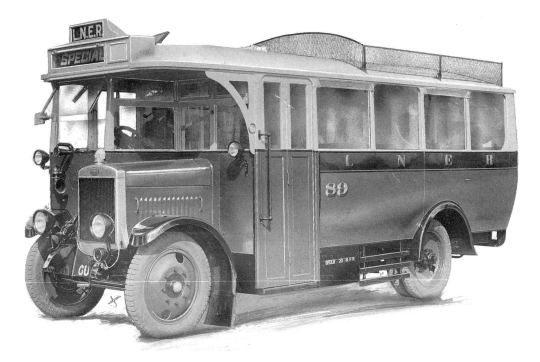

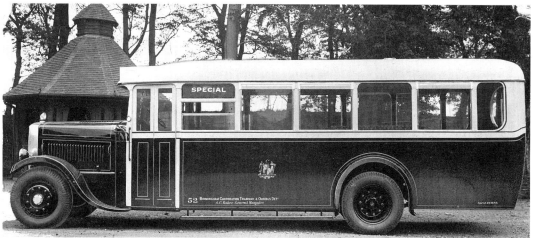

were introduced in 1928, as were single and double-deck four-wheel models. These last were later renamed Conquest (single-deck) and Invincible (double-deck). Buyers of the six-wheelers included the corporations of Birmingham, Hull, Leicester, Middlesbrough, Morecambe, Northampton, Oldham, Reading, Salford and Wolverhampton.

The Arab name was first used in 1933 for a much revised Conquest and Invincible range, covering both single and double-deck chassis. They were probably the first UK chassis specifically designed for Gardner oil engines, and were of relatively simple layout, with the crash gearbox still mounted half-way along the chassis rather than in unit with the engine. Double-deck chassis could take either 5LW or 6LW engines, while single-deckers were offered in both normal and

Above:
Two vehicles delivered in 1929 to two fleet operators showed different thinking. That for the London & North Eastern Railway *(top)* is one of 12 forward-control ONDs seating 20, while the other *(above)* is one of 30 normal-control Conquests with 25 seats supplied to Birmingham Corporation. The latter were used as tram replacements and were soon rebuilt to forward-control.
Author's Collection (both)

forward-control forms for 4LW or 5LW engines. However, sales were disappointing and more or less faded away completely in the mid-1930s. After that date Guy began to pick-up military contracts and perhaps was not too bothered. However, Burton-on-

Trent Corporation continued to support the single-deck Arab, starting with two normal-control models with Brush 26-seat bodies and 4LW engines in 1934, moving to forward-control 32-seaters in 1935, still with 4LWs, and buying more in 1940-41.

Guy was rather more successful with smaller models. Its low-cost OND and ONDF one-man buses offered between 1929 and 1931 had four-cylinder Meadows petrol engines. The F stood for forward-control. An unusual feature was the option of central or offside gear lever; the latter could be easier for one-man operation. A lengthened version was later added to the range. From 1933 until 1940 there were four models with different wheelbases but the same 3.3 litre petrol engines. Two sizes of Wolf (for 14 and 20 passengers) were normal-control, while both Vixens (24 and 26 passengers) were forward-control. The Wolfs (or Wolves?) operated by the small municipalities of Llandudno and Colwyn Bay were well known to holidaymakers.

It was World War 2 that put Guy back into big buses. After normal bus production had ended it was realised by the Government that there was an urgent need for simple, reliable buses to help carry workers to war factories. Originally Leyland and Guy were selected to build initial batches of 500 full-size double-deckers, but it was then decided that Leyland had more important military commitments, whereas cancellation of an order for searchlight-carrying trailers meant that there would be capacity at Guy. Sidney Guy turned down the offer of use of the drawings for Bristol's 'K'-type with Gardner engine and instead redesigned the 1933 Arab. The frame was new as was the front end, but the double-plate clutch and the crash gearbox with its gear positions the reverse of normal were pure 1933 (or earlier). Bonnet and dash design were very similar to Leyland's TD7 to meet ministry requirements for standardised dimensions for bodybuilders, and the frame even had the same profile as the TD7. The chassis was relatively heavy, since use of scarce lightweight materials such as aluminium was prohibited.

Most utility Arabs had the 7 litre Gardner 5LW engine, but some operators in hilly districts were permitted the larger 6LW. The prototype was completed in March 1942 and Swindon Corporation was the first to operate the type. By December 1944, 2,000 Arab chassis had been completed. They proved reliable and longlived despite the lack of sophistication. After conditions returned to normal, Guy was able to obtain repeat business from many of its enforced users.

Halley

Once as well known and as successful as Albion, Halley went into a long and painful decline, with local rival Albion subsequently buying the empty factory and reusing some of Halley's model names. Ironically, Halley had begun in the workshop where Albion had started. George Halley was the moving force in his company, and it was his long illness contracted when in his 30s that led to his death and ultimately the collapse of his company. George Halley's Glasgow Motor Lorry Co began building steam, then petrol, lorries in the old Albion workshop from 1900. Halley's Industrial Motors was set up in 1906 and subsequently moved to purpose-built premises. By 1910 it was also building its own engines. Most chassis were for goods carrying or fire appliances, but charabancs were also built, including some with six-cylinder engines. The first two buses for the newly-formed United Automobile in 1912 were Halleys and went into service at Lowestoft driven by two Glaswegian drivers. World War 1 production of Halleys was not only of chassis, but also included axles and gearbox parts for AEC.

The early postwar years saw a misguided attempt to sell only chassis with six-cylinder engines, a brand-new engine the company had spent much time and more money developing. The chassis was the 'P'-type, a 29-35-seat bus or a 3$\frac{1}{2}$-ton goods vehicle. The one model policy was a disaster and, ultimately, four-cylinder engines were reintroduced. The company was relatively quick to offer the option of normal or forward control on its models. By 1925, ironically, six-cylinder engines were in vogue for coaches and charabancs, but in 1927 the bank appointed a receiver.

A new company, Halley Motors, was formed and continued building on a smaller scale, a total staff of 100 contrasting with the 1,000 once employed. The same year saw the appearance of a six-wheel PSV,

The Commercial Motor Co began running this chain-drive Hallford in 1908. Makers J. & E. Hall repossessed it and proceeded to run the Maidstone-Gravesend service itself when the operator got into difficulties. Later W. F. French — the well-known pioneer — acquired the service and its buses. They subsequently became part of Maidstone & District. *Ian Allan Library*

the Security Six, at the Olympia Show. It was offered in normal and forward-control forms; two of the latter were sold. The well-known Harry Ricardo helped with engine design in the late 1920s and considerable improvements resulted. The Conqueror was a new forward-control, low-frame PSV perhaps named more in hope than reality. It did, however, achieve reasonable sales; for example, Scottish General Omnibus Co, later merged with Walter Alexander, bought six.

A six-cylinder engine was offered in the Neptune, a double-decker, and in its single-deck version, the Clansman. The Neptune was offered at the time when big orders for double-deckers were in the offing from Glasgow Corporation, but the operator was more hard-headed than patriotic, with AEC and Leyland doing well, but not Halley (or Albion).

There were still users of some size: Keith & Boyle (London), which owned Orange Luxury Coaches, had quite a fleet — but it also ran Halley's London sales operation; W. & R. Dunlop's Motor Service of Greenock, later taken over by Western SMT, was faithful to the marque, buying Conquerors with Duple

bodies up to 1936. Surprisingly, the North British Locomotive Co bought Halley in 1930, perhaps seeking to diversify, but it put no money into the business. Halley gave up building in 1935, although some already-completed chassis did not enter service until the following year.

Hallford and Hallford-Stevens

J. & E. Hall of Dartford is still a well-known name in refrigeration and engineering, but for 16 years the company also built buses and trucks. The early vehicles had chain drive, four-speed gearboxes and Hall-built engines to Saurer patents. A W. Austen ran three, with double-deck bodies, between Maidstone and Chatham but could not make the route pay. By 1911 Hallfords used the company's own design of engine. Wartime production was all lorry, and vehicle production ceased in 1925.

In association with W. A. Stevens of Maidstone, Hallford also provided the chassis and engine for Hallford-Stevens petrol-electrics, a predecessor of the Tillings-Stevens.

International

International Harvester's origins are revealed by its name. From 1907 it built cars of unusual mechanical layout with large wheels, and followed with goods carrying chassis. The layout eventually became orthodox. In 1928 a batch of its Six-Speed Special chassis were built with right-hand drive for export to the UK and possibly elsewhere. They still reflected

the company's farming origins in having high ground clearance and there was a two-speed rear-axle. They were quite small vehicles and were probably used in the UK as PSV chassis for station or hotel buses. Earlier, in 1925, SMT had three 14-seaters for its North Berwick service; they ran for four years.

Total production of the Space Six in the USA for 1928-29 was 49,020, a volume that offered enormous advantages of scale. But the benefits were shortly to be lost by the imposition of import duties in the UK. Surprisingly, one Speed Six survives in the UK.

Jackson

R. Reynold Jackson & Co of Notting Hill Gate, London, made cars for a number of years. However, in 1906 the company built a bus chassis. This was fitted with a 30hp Gnome engine and a wide steel chassis frame. Engine and gearbox were supported on a sub-frame hung from the main one. The three-speed gearbox was said to be made from gunmetal.

Karrier

Clayton & Co (Huddersfield) was a family firm which began building commercial vehicles with Tylor engines in 1908. The first passenger-carrying chassis appeared in 1910. They were sold as Karrier Cars and

Above:
Internationals were probably the most popular small buses run by the numerous small operators in Dublin in the late 1920s and early 1930s. Later, Morning Star, the operator of this example, merged with others working the O'Connell Bridge-Bray service to form a consortium. *Geoff Lumb Collection*

Below:
A 22-seat Karrier of the Pontypridd A. G. & Motor Car Co is seen with hood stowed for fine-weather travel. The high floor did not help stability on poor roads. *Author's Collection*

some 11 undertakings were named as operators in a 1912 catalogue. The following year saw a separate brochure of 'Karrier Cars for passenger services' with pictures of 16 different models including a double-decker.

Introduction of a 3-4-ton truck to meet the War Department's subsidy specification ultimately led to wartime production of such vehicles in quantity. The War Office also impressed other Karrier chassis due for delivery, including two chain-driven buses for the London & South Western Railway at Exeter; their replacements were also commandeered, but the third pair built to fulfil the order were finally delivered just before and just after Christmas 1914. A new, larger

Left:
Marlow & District had begun in 1925 and when Thames Valley gained control in 1929 ran 12 buses; all but one were Karriers. This fact was not surprising given that the controlling director was R. F. Clayton, who also controlled Karrier and who had a riverside home at Marlow. Most of the buses were CL4 models. *Arthur Ingram Collection*

works was built during the war, and later expanded. A new company, Karrier Motors, was formed in 1920 to take over the business. Karrier, like other makes, also rehabilitated ex-WD lorry chassis, and James Hodson, the predecessor of Ribble Motors, fitted four with open-top double-deck bodies. Over the next few years a number of new models were introduced, starting with the 'K'-type, which was a development of the wartime model. Others were the 'H'-type of 1922 for 20-26-seat bodywork, the smaller 'C'-type (1923) with Dorman engine, and the 14-seater (one-ton) 'Z'-type (1924).

Above:
Typical of the impressive looking buses produced by Karrier in the late 1920s is this DD6 for Wallasey Corporation. It seated 66 and was one of six bought in 1928, the same year that Wallasey also bought some early Leyland Titans. The Karriers remained in the fleet for barely three years, the Leylands rather longer. *Geoff Lumb Collection*

A 1923 Commercial Motor Show exhibit was a 50-seater articulated vehicle, the front part being a 'K'-type tractive unit, the rear a 50-seat semi-trailer with self-steering rear axle. Unfortunately, even the limited legislation of the time did not permit its use as a PSV. A new passenger range in 1925 was the 'KL', with low-height chassis and pneumatic tyres, features which were copied by the Leyland PLSC Lion a year later. Unfortunately, Leyland seemed to have the resources or abilities to achieve a degree of reliability that eluded Karrier.

The 1925 Show saw the unveiling of the first six-wheeler, the Karrier WL6, with a platform height of only 2ft (600mm) and extravagant claims of better riding, greater safety, better braking, reduced wheel-spin, reduced tractive effort, fuel and tyre economy, and reduced maintenance costs! An even lower frame height of 1ft 9¼in (520mm) was achieved on the CL4 by cranking the main side-members of the chassis frame under the back axles. In just under seven years' production nearly 90 were sold, with either Dorman or Karrier's own engine fitted. Another six-wheeler followed at the end of 1926. This, the CL6, had the frame cranked over the rear axles. It was of a lighter build, officially for 32 passengers against the 40 of the WL6, and had a smaller Dorman engine. Production of CL6s was around 50, while WL6 (and WL6/1 with longer wheelbase) accounted for 160.

Double-deck sales reached some 40 of the three-axle WL6/2, plus another 23 DD6 or DD6/1. A Karrier sleeve-valve engine was fitted to many. The engine's distinguishing features included a separate oil cooler under the radiator and the flywheel, which was in the centre of the six-cylinder engine — in other words, between the third and fourth pistons. Karrier saw a great future for the six-wheeler and for some years had devoted much of its design efforts in this direction. Liverpool Corporation had over 80 of the type, while the corporations of Edinburgh, Oldham, Portsmouth and Salford each had 15 or 16. However, Edinburgh, having bought 14 WL6/1 single-deckers in 1927-28, found them unreliable; its last had gone by 1932. Axle and spring location and stresses and strains, particularly of double drives, were insufficiently understood, and Karrier gained a poor reputation for reliability generally. In addition, such vehicles were heavy in weight and had a high fuel consumption. By 1929 sales of six-wheelers were plummeting.

Later models were all two-axle, with four-wheel brakes ultimately becoming standard. The JKL, later renamed Chaser 4, was the most successful, and later a Chaser 6 was added for those wanting a faster vehicle. The best-known Chaser was the road/rail one built for the London, Midland & Scottish Railway. More mundane were two Chaser 6s for local operator Huddersfield Joint Omnibus Committee. These were fitted with Gardner 6LW diesel engines.

The last new passenger model was the Monitor, although few were sold. The recession, competition from AEC and Leyland, and the move to diesel engines were too much. As a result Karrier got into financial difficulties. There was an abortive plan to merge with TSM to try and survive.

In 1931 the company had 7% of the municipal bus market; two years later bus building ceased and in 1934 Rootes took it over, moving truck production to Luton the following year.

Lacoste et Battman

This French car and component maker built complete commercial vehicle chassis for a short time. London & Provincial Bus & Traction Co, whose fleetname was Arrow, ran a fleet of this make in 1906, and various other London operators tried one or two. All were of conventional layout with 34-seat open-top bodies. When Liverpool Corporation Tramways began bus operation in 1911 (by taking over a smaller operator) one of its four buses was of this make.

Lacre

Best-known as a maker of road-sweeping equipment, Lacre had a large range of models on offer by 1909 and in 1910 opened at Letchworth, Hertfordshire, what was claimed to be the first purpose-built plant in the UK for the manufacture of commercial vehicles. The first two years of World War 1 saw all production as military vehicles for Belgium, after which some chassis were bodied for passenger use. Crosville had a Lacre charabanc in 1913 and in 1916 bought some bus-bodied examples. Ultimately the operator had 10 Lacres in its fleet.

Laffly

French maker Laffly built chassis under the Laffly-Schneider name from 1922 and under the Laffly name from 1925; specific bus models were soon added.

Lambourn

Lambourn Garages, of Lambourn, Berkshire, in conjunction with Universal Power Drives, of Perivale, Middlesex, built a number of horseboxes under the Lambourn name in the late 1930s. The vehicles had a Fordson V8 petrol engine mounted low down at the rear of the chassis. In 1937 a passenger-carrying version was produced. It had a similar layout, complete with dummy Fordson radiator grille at the front and a real radiator at the rear behind the engine. Many other components, such as gearbox and clutch, were Fordson-derived. Throttle and clutch were hydraulically operated, and the remote gear control was by cable. Between-axles chassis frame height was low, just 18in (450mm).

Lancia

The old-established Italian vehicle builder Lancia first exhibited in Britain at the 1921 Olympia Show, subsequently becoming one of the more successful importers of the 1920s. The biggest operator must have been the Barton business, with 100 bought new or secondhand. Some of the Barton examples were ex-World War 1 chassis acquired from the government in Italy. Many of the Lancias became Lancia-Bartons and had greatly extended chassis. These were fitted with an additional axle, a Barton practice that was also applied to other makes.

Genuine Lancias featured in many other fleets as charabancs and had a reputation for high speeds.

Latil

The old-established French maker Latil had considerable success in the UK in the 1930s with a four-wheel drive heavy duty tractive unit built under licence by Shelvoke & Drewry. In the previous decade it had sold a few PSVs in the UK. These included, for example, a 1924 14-seat bus which operated for 10 years with Midland Bus Services and its successor, Western SMT, while the Southern National Omnibus Co also acquired a 14-seater when it took over a small operator's four-vehicle fleet in 1935.

Below:
Lancia chassis sold well in the UK in the 1920s, to a variety of operators; the Pentaiota was particularly popular as a charabanc. Barton Bros ran some Lancias in standard form and also lengthened others. Further examples were extended even more, gaining a third, trailing, axle at the same time — as shown here. The much rebuilt chassis were generally known as Lancia-Bartons. *Arthur Ingram Collection*

Leyland

Of all the bus manufacturers Leyland was undoubtedly the most successful. It built the most vehicles and successfully developed some of the most advanced designs. But it was not without hard times. The decision to buy back Government surplus World War 1 Leylands and recondition them before sale (to protect the company's reputation) almost bankrupted it and, at a later date, the bank felt obliged to put in its own manager to run the company.

If there is one legendary model it is, of course, the original Titan designed by G. J. Rackham. But after he left (and he did not stay long) Leyland kept up the momentum, constantly improving the Titan and the other models. Some pre-Titan models were very successful too, such as the Lion.

Leyland had originated as a steam vehicle builder in 1896 (having previously produced steam lawnmowers), becoming the Lancashire Steam Motor Co, but after 11 years changed its name to Leyland Motors to reflect the greater number of petrol-engined vehicles being produced. It had been among the earlier steam builders to see the limitations of this form of propulsion and had begun to develop its own petrol engines, although initially those vehicles sold were fitted by engines of Crossley manufacture. The 'X'-type of 1907, a $3^1/_2$ tonner for lorry or bus use, was probably the first model with an engine entirely of Leyland design.

The company was also early in offering four-speed gearboxes, with the top ratio giving direct drive. Smaller models were soon added, with smaller engines. Another range of engines followed in 1909.

Cast aluminium was used for the crankcase and other parts, and both sets of valves were on the same side.

In 1912 Leyland became the only maker to receive War Office approval for both $1^1/_2$ and 3 tonners in its subsidy scheme. This scheme enabled buyers to receive an annual payment for buying and keeping in good condition vehicles of approved design which could be repurchased at a premium in the event of war. Although applying to goods vehicles, the scheme boosted sales generally and the chassis were the same anyway. When war broke out in 1914 not only goods vehicles were requisitioned, but also bus chassis (which were not in the scheme). Edinburgh Corporation had just bought its first three buses, but the War Department took them, and many others from elsewhere.

The models became known as subsidy models, which Leyland went on to build in huge numbers; nearly 6,000 went to the Royal Flying Corps (forerunner of the Royal Air Force) in four years. These became known as the RAF type. About half were bought back by Leyland after the war and reconditioned in a factory at Kingston, Surrey, over a five-year period. But sales of these (and other ex-WD makes) did nothing to help new chassis sales, and at

Below:
Haslingden Corporation was an early municipal bus operator, and bought this Leyland-bodied Leyland 'X'-type in 1907. The 'X' was a $3^1/_2$ ton model and the first successful petrol-engined vehicle. It had a new four-cylinder six-litre engine with 'T' cylinder head that developed 40hp. *Author's Collection*

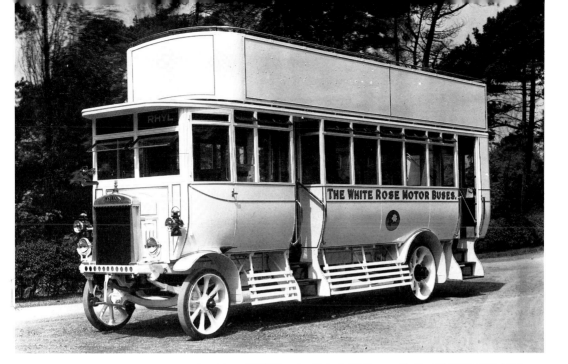

Above:
The 'SG' range sold in quantity as single and double-deckers in the early 1920s. The White Rose fleet of Brookes Bros of Rhyl took several; note the oil sidelights. Crosville later took over the 87-strong Brookes fleet. *Ian Allan Library*

Right:
Leyland was envious of AEC's monopoly in London, and developed a special light version of its G7 chassis to meet Metropolitan Police requirements. It was fitted with three independent brakes and a quiet four-speed gearbox. The pioneer London independent, Arthur Partridge's Chocolate Express, bought the first, in 1922, for £1,600 complete with Dodson body. He paid a deposit of £530 and the balance plus 5% interest in 12 monthly payments of £93 12s (£93.60). *Author's Collection*

Right:
Leyland's Titans, and other models that copied it, with their overall height much lower than before and a lower centre of gravity, allowed operators to run double-deckers into rural areas and on long inter-urban routes. This early Titan of Maidstone & District was photographed in Ightham, Kent, in 1936. *Author's Collection*

one stage in the early 1920s the Lancashire factory was working only four days in a fortnight. It was the bus sales that kept the company afloat, and between 1922 and 1924 these doubled each year.

A big range of new chassis, of varying sizes and capacities, had been announced fairly soon after the war ended. The 'N'-type, with 36-40hp engine and worm rear axle was the most popular for bus use, with Southdown being one big buyer. Southdown was also a buyer for the 'G'-range that quickly followed, buying more than 50 of the type over five years. The next design step, in 1922, was to move the driver alongside the engine to provide more room for passengers within a given length. Leyland called such vehicles 'side type' and added an S to the type name; thus an SG7 was a forward-control G7.

The first purpose-built bus chassis came in 1925 with five new models, all beginning with the letter 'L'. The double-deck Leviathan sold in reasonable numbers, the bonneted Lioness sold better, and the forward-control single-deck Lion sold exceptionally well; local operator Ribble bought over 180 Lions between 1926 and 1928. Chassis frame height of the 'L' models was about one foot (30cm) lower than their predecessors, largely because of a better method of attaching the axles to the frame. Most (but not the double-decker) had pneumatic tyres.

The fact that Leyland built bodies as well as chassis was of enormous benefit in developing the Titan, which was announced in 1927. Its overall height as a closed-top double-decker was about two feet (60cm) lower than the Leviathan and probably nearer three feet (90cm) lower than some other makes. The drop-frame chassis was not new, but Leyland also ran the propshaft along the nearside of the chassis (instead of along the centre line) so that the central gangway in the lower deck could be lower than the floor level under the seats, to gain a valuable inch or so. Instead of a centre gangway upstairs, seats were grouped in fours towards the nearside, with a sunken (or dropped) gangway on the offside. It intruded into the lower deck where passengers using the seats nearest the windows on the offside had to be careful to duck when entering or leaving their seats. All this produced an overall height of just 12ft 10in (3.91m). Careful body design, including use of aluminium panels, kept weight down and enabled pneumatic tyres to be used. The other big surprise with the Titan was its new six-cylinder overhead camshaft engine, with gearbox directly bolted to it. With improvements and modifications, the petrol engine was to remain in production until 1948, and it also formed the basis of the first Leyland production diesel engine. Vacuum-servo brakes were another feature of the Titan. Almost all the features of the Titan chassis were repeated on its single-deck counterpart, the Tiger, and there was also a three-axle double-decker, the Titanic, which sold in tiny numbers.

From the announcement of the first Titans the story became one of successive improvements up to the mid-1930s, after which the pace slackened a little. The most significant event was the development of Leyland's own diesel engine, initially of 8.1 litre capacity and later 8.6. It was based on the petrol engine, and that too was increased in capacity and subsequently received a top-end redesign. Take up of petrol engines in double-deckers soon dwindled, with notable exceptions such as Bournemouth Corporation, but Ribble kept to petrol engines in single-deckers, surprisingly, and smaller coach operators generally preferred them. Final 'prewar' models of the Tiger and Titan families were not actually announced until after the outbreak of war in September 1939.

Reverting to the late 1920s, many of the Titan/Tiger improvements could also be found on new versions of the Lion and Lioness. There was a four-cylinder version of the new six-cylinder engine, and the Lion continued to sell well as a lighter alternative for other than the busiest urban bus services. These models retained the central transmission line, and so were slightly higher off the ground. Lions were redesigned in 1934, gaining a 5.7 litre diesel option, along with a more upright front end. The shorter engine permitted an extra row of seats to be fitted into the bodywork so that, ironically, the smaller-engined vehicle had the higher passenger capacity.

The Kingston works, once used for rebuilding World War 1 Leylands, was re-equipped from 1931 to build a new light range of normal-control goods and passenger chassis, the latter for 20-seat bodywork, with a new 4.4 litre petrol engine. Subsequently, forward-control models were also offered, and a 4.4 litre diesel option (later enlarged to 4.7 litres) was also available.

Leyland did not follow the AEC/Daimler path by

Left:
The Cheetah, announced in 1935, was a lightweight designed for light bodywork and for economy. Most of its parts were a mix of Cub or Lion. The SMT group bought 300 with diesel engines and full-fronted bodywork, while Ribble took slightly more over a four-year period, all petrol-engined. This one in Alexander colours never ran for the operator; all of the intended batch were diverted to Western SMT. *Author's Collection*

Centre left:
There was a resurgence of interest in three-axle buses in the mid to late 1930s. Central SMT and Western SMT between them took 38 of these three-axle Tiger TS6Ts, while City Coach Co took some 36. City had a Wood Green-Southend stage service that was incredibly busy at summer weekends yet was limited to single-deckers — so the extra capacity was useful. *Author's Collection*

Below:
The Tiger FEC underfloor-engined chassis — note the nearside radiator. What appears to be a conventional gear lever is the selector for the pre-selector gearbox, as also found on AEC Regents and Regals supplied to London. Leyland obviously still kept an eye on America, for it described the FEC as 'the forerunner of a British transit bus'. *Author's Collection*

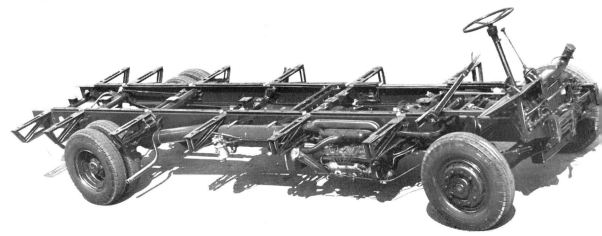

offering pre-selector gearboxes, but instead developed the torque convertor, which virtually eliminated gear changing; above about 20mph a driver just moved a lever to select direct drive. Offered from 1933 in a range of chassis, the 'gearless bus' transmission sold well, particularly to municipal operators replacing trams or those with hilly territory, or both. As an automatic transmission it was a pioneering effort, years ahead of any other. But there was a penalty in the higher fuel consumption, and sales dropped off in the late 1930s.

One new model in the mid-1930s was the Cheetah, a full-sized forward-control chassis that was a cross between a Lion and a Cub, with a light six-cylinder engine. Practically none were sold for export, which suggests that Leyland realised that performance was questionable unless the unladen weight was strictly adhered to. Even so, several hundred were sold, notably in Scotland, while Ribble was unusual in specifying petrol engines. Technically, they provided an interesting contrast with the Lion with its four-cylinder engine, which still continued in production.

War cut short another promising development — the underfloor-engined single-decker of which 88 were built for London Transport. The layout subsequently became standard for single-deckers in the UK, and was developed with LT. It reflected one of the lessons that LT had learnt with the AEC 'Q' — the desirability of keeping every mechanical part below floor level.

Leyland bus production gradually diminished in 1940, though subsequently under Government direction it completed a large number of Titans and Tigers on which construction work had started before being halted by the war.

Lifu

The copper boiler must have made a Lifu steam bus a particularly impressive — and expensive — vehicle. The name stood for Liquid Fuel Engineering Co, a company which was based at Cowes on the Isle of Wight. The company was building steam cars and trucks before 1900. A road train was used to collect and deliver parcels in and around Swindon for a syndicate which included the Midland & South Western Junction Railway; in the summer of 1898 a 20-seat car was added as a second trailer and began working between Cirencester and Fairford. The following summer the road train ran again, this time from Cirencester to Fairford, Lechlade and Faringdon. Another Lifu, a steam bus, started a Torquay-Paignton service in 1899. At that year's Agricultural Hall Motor Show, Lifu exhibited a 28-seat double-decker and a wagonette. However, the Cowes works closed in 1900.

The Scottish Motor Traction Co, having laid down a performance specification for potential suppliers, ordered two Lifus in 1905 through a Wishaw company. But after a short trial they were rejected for lack of power, presumably because they could not reach the required 12mph on the level or 3mph on a 1 in 6 gradient. They were no doubt built by another contractor under licence as the Lifu works had closed, but must have involved somebody in considerable expense. Some Belhavens were also built under Lifu patents and, ironically, SMT also tried and rejected one of these.

London General

The London General Omnibus Co began building its own buses with the 'X'-type in 1909, and continued with the famous 'B'-type in the following year. The buses were constructed at the Walthamstow overhaul works which had originally been used by Vanguard. After the Underground Group obtained control of the LGOC there was a change of policy and Walthamstow became a separate entity, the Associated Equipment Co — better known as AEC.

'High quality of parts and interchangeability' were the maxim for the 'B'-type, according to Walter Iden, who was joint designer with Frank Searle. From employing 300-400 workers in an overhaul shop

Right:
London General built its 'X'-type at Walthamstow and later went on to construct the legendary 'B'-type there. This is an early 'X'-type.
Author's Collection

A strange final episode was the decision to design and build at Chiswick six four-wheel single-deckers (type 'CB') and six six-wheel double-deckers (type 'CC'); the numbers were reduced at a late stage and only three single-deckers and four double-deckers were completed, in 1931 and 1932. By this stage the LGOC was heavily committed to AEC's new Regal, Regent and Renown types. The final Chiswick-built buses used mainly proprietary units, including Kirkstall axles and Meadows petrol engines. They later gained some AEC components, but all were withdrawn by 1940.

which also manufactured spare parts, Walthamstow went on to employ between 3,000 and 4,000. Production of new chassis ran at a regular 30 a week, but at one stage the addition of a night shift pushed the figure to 60. Some 'B'-type bodies were also built at Walthamstow.

Years later, in the mid-1920s, the LGOC's new Chiswick works assembled considerable numbers of 'NS'-type buses, the parts for which were produced by AEC at Walthamstow. Chiswick also built eight all-weather touring coaches in 1926, fitting Daimler sleeve-valve engines along with 'NS' back axles and brakes.

Lothian

Nearly 100 Lothians were built by the Scottish Motor Traction Co between 1913 and 1924. Like some other operators, SMT was not satisfied with what was commercially available at the time. A few chassis were supplied to other Scottish operators, and a number of chassis were originally built as trucks. Nearly all chassis were forward-control, unusual at that time, and took full-front bodywork. The vehicles were bodied as either single or double-deckers. The first chassis had Minerva engines and later ones had Tylor units; a chain-driven gearbox was standard.

M & D

Just one model was offered by this mid-1920s maker, a four-cylinder engined chassis suitable for 14-seat bodywork. However, it did have brakes on all four wheels. It was sold by a Birmingham company.

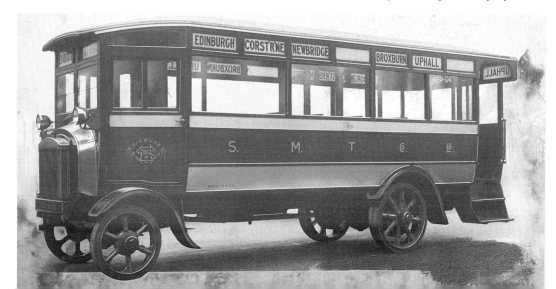

Maltby

Beginning as a bodybuilder, Maltby's Motor Works of Sandgate, Kent, expanded into producing complete vehicles. All were charabancs and constructed in small numbers for local operators. Production lasted for some 15 years before the company reverted to bodybuilding, mainly for cars. The earliest models had Coronet engines built in Coventry by one Walter Iden (later to become general manager and chief engineer of AEC at the same time as remaining chief engineer of the LGOC). Later Maltby charabancs were fitted with White and Poppe engines. A 40hp Maltby ordered by F. W. Wacher & Co passed straight to East Kent Road Car, having been delivered after the former company was taken over.

Manchester

In the late 1920s Willys-Overland-Crossley assembled Willys-Overlands for the British market. However, the company also made its own design of 1.25 and 1.75 ton trucks, which were of typical North American design with such features as spiral-bevel back axle and coil ignition. They were later badged as Willys-Manchester or Manchester, and the larger model was also offered as a 14-seat PSV. Seven Manchesters went into the LPTB fleet in 1933 when small operators were compulsorily acquired.

Martin

An unlikely producer of bus chassis was the Martin Cultivator Co of Stamford, Lincolnshire. It built farm

tractors and trailer fire pumps, but briefly in the mid-1920s produced a fire engine and — probably — just one PSV chassis.

Maudslay

The fortunes of the Maudslay Motor Co of Coventry see-sawed in remarkable fashion. Twice, when the company was in a critical condition, it staged a comeback with advanced and innovative designs. Its pedigree was of the finest. Henry Maudslay was a pioneer of the industrial revolution. He made the first screw-cutting lathe, which made it possible for screw threads to be standardised, and he made the first micrometer which opened up developments leading to modern ideas of production engineering. His great-grandson founded the Maudslay Motor Co at the beginning of this century.

A number of 12-seat buses powered by two-cylinder overhead-valve engines of 2.4 litre were supplied to the Great Western Railway in 1905 and the same year saw a double-deck chassis with four-cylinder 6.4 litre engine with equal bore and stroke. The engine had an overhead camshaft on a hinged frame so that a valve could be changed in a claimed two minutes. One of these buses, with sliding mesh

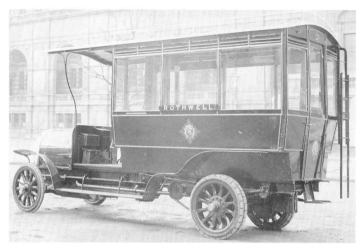

gearbox and chain drive, inaugurated operations of the Scottish Motor Traction Co in Edinburgh in 1906.

World War 1 saw production of models to government-approved subsidy design, and Maudslays were also built by the Rover Co. Improved models came out after the war with detachable cylinder heads but without swing-over camshafts. However, times were difficult, with so many ex-War Department vehicles on the market.

Autumn 1924 saw the first dedicated PSV chassis, the four-cylinder 'ML'-type, with a low frame, a concept introduced by AEC only the previous year. Engines were mounted in a subframe with the separate gearbox inclined downwards towards the rear to give a straight transmission line to the underslung worm-driven back axle. Normal and forward-control models were offered, with six-cylinder engines added

to the options in 1927. The range remained in production (with improvements) until 1936. A low-frame version of the less successful double-deck chassis came in 1925.

Particular sales successes were with the GWR and SMT, the latter buying 165 Maudslays between 1925 and 1929. Regrouping in the bus industry saw the growing Crosville Motor Services swallow Western Transport of Wrexham in 1933 and its fleet which included 16 ex-GWR Maudslays, while others of the make were amongst another part of the GWR fleet transferred to Thames Valley Traction. Events such as these meant that by the early 1930s Maudslays sold mainly to independents, with the likes of AEC, Bristol and Leyland achieving great successes with the larger operators.

Dwindling sales prompted Maudslay's other big

leap forward in design, the high capacity SF40, later named the Magna. Introduced in 1935, it had a conventional vertical engine and radiator, but the front axle was moved rearwards sufficiently to allow the entrance to be placed forward of it. Up to 40 seats could be accommodated in a bus built to the then maximum length of 27ft 6in (8.38m). Engine and gearbox were still in a subframe, now slightly flexibly mounted, and the relatively high chassis permitted a straight transmission line. Many of the units were similar to those of the 'MLs', and there was also a new conventional single-decker, the ML5, with a neater and more compact front end. It was later named Marathon; this and the Magna were offered with Maudslay's 5.43 litre petrol engine or with Gardner 4LW or 5LW diesel.

Maxwell

This American maker from Detroit had made cars for a few years, then added vans and trucks from about the end of World War 1 until 1925. The chassis were mostly car-derived, as with many other makes, with a lengthened frame and changed gear ratio. Such chassis could carry bodies for up to 14 seats. The National Motor Museum at Beaulieu has a 21hp charabanc in its collection.

McCurd

The name might sound Scottish, but W. A. McCurd was a London car dealer. In 1912 he introduced a commercial vehicle chassis which was built in his own premises, and was unusual for the time in having a worm-driven back axle. Harrogate Road Car liked the design, taking its ninth in 1919. Southdown bought a couple of McCurds in 1915, no doubt because they were of no interest to the War Office and therefore were still available.

The original factory was at Cricklewood, but production seems to have ceased for a time before recommencing from premises at Hayes in Middlesex in the mid-1920s. The company then offered a PSV chassis with four-wheel brakes. Then followed another move, to Slough, by which time the company had become McCurd Motors and offered a respectable normal-control chassis with drop frame and pneumatic tyres for up to 26 seats. McCurds at one stage certainly manufactured more of its own components than most, but by 1927 competition was just too great and production ceased.

Mercedes-Benz

Chassis built by Mercedes-Benz have never been numerous in the UK, but a limited number were sold in the late 1920s and early 1930s. One notable operation were two pioneer express services run by Pullman Roadways of Croydon; the company ran daily London-Southampton-Bournemouth and London-Torquay-Plymouth routes with a fleet of five 20-seat Mercedes-Benz luxury coaches. Both routes started from Croydon before heading to London.

Mercedes-Benz exhibits at the 1929 Olympia

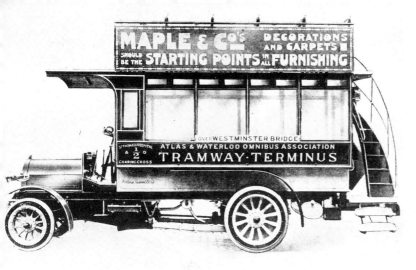

Motor Show were a normal-control 20-seater with six-cylinder engine and another normal-control model for up to 32 seats. The company was early in the field with diesel engines, a Midlands operator being among the first, in September 1930, to order one for a coach.

The company rather faded from the scene after 1931, but briefly reappeared in 1938 with a forward-control model said to seat up to 44 passengers.

Milnes and Milnes-Daimler

Best known of the early motorbus builders was undoubtedly Milnes-Daimler, formed from as association between an important British tramcar builder (Milnes) and Daimler Motoren Gesellschaft of Canstatt, Wurtenburg, Germany. By 1907 the company had become by far the largest provider of motorbuses, with over 600 in service in Britain. It had started, however, with lorries made by Milnes and fitted with German Daimler engines. The first bus came in 1902; it went to Portsmouth & Gosport Motors. Later that year the Milnes-Daimler company was formed. The company later also sold Mercedes cars. One of the directors was H. G. Burford, who was later to set up his own company, which initially imported vehicles from a different continent. Once the boom in tramway building and electrification was over, the Milnes tramcar-building business went into liquidation, but luckily left Milnes-Daimler more or less unaffected. However, the company subsequently sold just chassis rather than the complete vehicles with Milnes bodies it had previously offered.

The Great Western Railway, the Great North of Scotland Railway and Eastbourne Corporation were all early operators. After the Vanguard and Road Car fleets merged with the LGOC there were over 300 Milnes-Daimlers in the combined fleet. The earliest Milnes-Daimlers had two-cylinder 20hp engines, with two change-speed (or gear) levers, and the brake and clutch were linked so that the clutch disconnected when the brakes were applied. That may have eased driving, but it probably contributed to the accident on Handcross Hill in 1906 when a Vanguard open-top double-decker on a run to Brighton ran out of control, killing eight passengers and retarding progress generally with longer distance bus services.

The Achilles' heel of what was generally a remarkably reliable bus for the time was the dead rear axle. Small pinions at the end of live drive shafts engaged with teeth cut internally around the inside of the wheel rim. It worked but was dreadfully noisy after wear and tear and dirt had taken their toll. In London the Metropolitan Police were always complaining about the noise and ordering noisy vehicles off the road.

By 1909 the company was selling Mercedes cars in some quantity, and enthusiasm for this, combined with competition from improved designs by other PSV builders, caused a big drop in bus sales. World War 1 and the German connection effectively killed the company; supply of chassis and components ceased and, in any event, few people would have wanted to buy. The company, by then named Milnes-Daimler-Mercedes, was wound up under the Trading with the Enemy (Amendment) Act in 1916.

Minerva

Based in Antwerp, Belgium, Minerva had begun with bicycles and developed through motorcycles to cars and trucks. Its first true passenger chassis were full-sized models produced in 1926, with 5.3 litre engines. Later engine size increased to 6.0 litre, but smaller PSVs seating 20 to 24 were added to the range. These were fitted with 3.6 litre engines.

When East Kent took over the Redbourn Group of coach operators in the Thanet area in 1935 it acquired nine Minervas. Some were normal-control models, others forward-control. They had been new between 1927 and 1931. Seating capacity varied from 26 to 31. All were soon sold, but few saw further service.

MOC

One of the first bus companies to build its own vehicles was the London Motor Omnibus Co, better known as Vanguard. It formed a subsidiary, Motor Omnibus Construction Ltd, which began to build double-deckers for it in 1906. MOC used Armstrong-

Whitworth engines, and some Armstrong-Whitworth buses in the Vanguard fleet were also badged MOC; there was a total of 20 of these two types in the fleet. Walthamstow went on to build the 'X' and 'B'-types under LGOC control, and later became the AEC works. Not every MOC went to Vanguard; Southdown's predecessor, the Sussex Motor Road Car Co, bought one in 1908 and fitted it with what became known as Mackenzie's slipper design of charabanc body (in which each row of transverse seats was 5in (12.5cm) higher than the one in front so that the rearmost passengers were seated very high up). Mackenzie was Southdown's traffic manager for many years.

Morris-Commercial

William Morris began building commercial vehicles in 1924. Although aimed mainly at the goods vehicle market, many of the 'T', 'TX' and 'Z'-types were bought for bus use. Then, in 1930, came purpose-built chassis, starting with the six-cylinder engined Viceroy (or 'Y'-type) and the Dictator (or 'H'-type). Two years later came the meritorious, but relatively unsuccessful, double-decker, the Imperial, of which just over 80 were built in two years. Local operator Birmingham Corporation took 50 and ultimately 30 went to East Kent.

Below:
Engine, gearbox and radiator of the single-deck Dictator and the double-deck Imperial could be easily disconnected and removed. However, adding this innovation probably increased cost. This Dictator carries a neat crew cab while undergoing a road test for *Modern Transport. Ian Allan Library*

A strange reversal of the usual pattern was the subsequent production of some bus chassis, such as the Dictator, as heavy trucks. A later bonneted single-decker was the Director (or 'RP'-type), a truck derivative, but with a drop frame and four-cylinder engine; both Aldershot & District and East Kent bought the model.

Of all the buses, the Dictator and Imperial were the most interesting. They were designed by chief engineer Charles K. Edwards, who had previously worked for AEC as chief designer. At a time when mechanical reliability was improving, the engine and gearbox plus radiator could be disconnected and wheeled out on the front axle. The cylinder head could be removed without disturbing the valve timing or camshaft drive and just three nuts secured the water pump.

Subsequently, heavy duty passenger chassis faded from the scene, although a new single-decker, based on the Equi-load truck, appeared in 1938.

Morton

General engineering company Robert Morton & Sons, of Wishaw, had built a few steam vehicles under licence from Lifu in the first years of this century. From 1907 construction was undertaken by a new company, Belhaven Engineering & Motors. One Morton is said to have received an open-top bus body seating 40, and to have been operated by the Caledonian Railway during 1906.

Napier

Napier is better remembered for its cars, racing cars and aero engines, but from time to time it offered commercial vehicles and passenger chassis. In 1901, the first year of the company's existence, a few charabancs were built on modified car chassis and a bus chassis was offered, briefly, five years later.

Commercial vehicle models were produced in a more serious manner from 1912, when a separate department was formed, but dropped altogether some 10 years later. Gearboxes on later models were mounted in unit with the engines.

Northern General

The few larger bus companies that saw a need to design and build chassis to meet their own special requirements generally began in the early part of this century. Northern General Transport, however, found itself in this position in the early 1930s. Traffic was growing, but parts of its territory were littered with low bridges which precluded the use of double-deckers on many routes. It needed modern, high capacity single-deckers.

This led to the production between 1933 and 1939 of some 67 side-engined single-deckers, of a chassis layout not unlike that of the AEC 'Q'-type. On all but the prototype the front axle was set back. All the petrol-engined buses, and some luxury coaches that were also built, had Hercules six-cylinder engines imported from America. These engines were particularly compact and led to less intrusion in the interior than on the 'Q'-type, which had to have a longitudinal offside seat above the engine. NGT managed to get all seats facing forward. The vehicles were 30ft (9.14m) long six-wheelers.

The chassis for the largest batch built, 31 in 1935, were assembled by AEC at Southall, and it has been suggested that this was some kind of deal to assuage AEC's complaint of patent infringement. Only one axle of the twin rear axle assembly was driven. The final 25 built, plus a prototype, were only 27ft 6in (8.38m) long with a single rear axle and seated 40.

Above:
This is a close-up of NGT's side-engined six-wheeler. Note how squat the US-built Hercules engine is, thereby creating minimal intrusion into the saloon of the bus. *Author's Collection*

Below:
A production version of NGT's SE6 which illustrates the type's set-back front axle. Unlike the AEC 'Q', the SE6 had a front-mounted radiator. Seating capacity was 44. *Author's Collection*

During World War 2 one of the 30ft-long buses was converted to two-axle, thus becoming the first of this configuration in the UK. The two-axle buses were built with diesel engines, a modified version of the new AEC 6.6 litre design, installed at an angle of 30°. Most of the petrol-engined buses were converted to diesel in later life, using AEC engines specially designed for the by then outdated Matilda tank. They were bought in pairs (as fitted to the tanks), and those with auxiliaries mounted on the offside of the engine went into the SE6s, while those with nearside ones were used to convert Midland Red-built SOS chassis that also featured in the NGT fleet.

Opel

Well known German maker Opel added trucks to its car and van range at a very early stage. Best known Opels of all were the Blitz range, introduced in 1931. The make sold in the UK in small numbers in the 1930s as an alternative to the Bedford and some remained in service into the postwar period, despite the obvious problem of spares.

Orion

Although built in Zurich, Switzerland, for only 11 years Orions were surprisingly successful in export markets. Five of these horizontal-engined buses were running in London during 1905, two with the LGOC and three with the Victoria Motor Omnibus Co. The first two buses of the Cambrian Railways were of this make and lasted from 1906 until 1912.

Overland

Willys Overland Crossley was an offshoot of Crossley Motors of Gorton, Manchester, and was set up in 1920 to assemble Willys-Overland vehicles for the UK. It later added models of its own designs,

albeit using US-sourced major components, and from 1928 these chassis were sold as Overland Manchesters. The 1.75 tonne truck of 1929 fitted with 3.6 litre five-bearing engine was also offered as a 14-seat coach. By 1933 the company had gone into liquidation.

Pagefield

Best remembered for its refuse collection system and vehicles, Pagefields were made by Walker Bros of Wigan, who were mining engineers. Cars, vans and lorries were also made plus a few buses around 1919/20 on lorry chassis. Then in 1927 a low-frame PSV chassis was introduced. Remarkably advanced for its time, it had a six-cylinder Dorman engine, four-wheel internally-expanding drum brakes, and sub-assemblies that were isolated from chassis flexing. The whole engine assembly could be easily detached and wheeled out, an idea followed a few years later by Morris-Commercial. However, the cone clutch was rather dated. Total PSV production was less than 10. Users included Grant's Saloon Services in Scotland and — more locally — Wigan Corporation.

Palladium

Originally a car maker, Palladium started building commercial vehicles in 1913, achieving some success with a Dorman-engined 3-4 ton chassis, a number of which were bodied as buses. An unusual feature of a

Below:
These two Swiss Orions, with bodies by Christopher Dodson of London, were the first two motorbuses owned by Cambrian Railways. They began running between Pwllheli and Nevin in 1906. *Author's Collection*

purpose-built coach chassis introduced at the 1920 Olympia Show was the option of double cantilever rear suspension. Road Motors of Luton, later taken over by National Omnibus & Transport, had a few of the type. One or two Palladiums were bodied as double-deckers. The maker was based in west London and closed down in 1924.

Peugeot

French maker Automobiles Peugeot had offered commercial vehicles from when it began production in 1894. In 1905 a 1^1/$_2$ ton truck with two-cylinder 1.8 litre engine was available in the UK at a price of £450. It was probably one of these that formed the basis of a 14-seat bus that ran between Fraserburgh, Rosehearty and New Aberdour in 1906.

Pickering

Tweedmouth, near Berwick-on-Tweed, was the unlikely location of this maker of commercial chassis. Established in 1905, it was claiming in 1906 that despite an annual output of 300 'it was kept more than fully engaged'. That too was unlikely; the company folded the same year.

One Pickering single-decker ran in Penrith, while another, a double-decker, was — just — an exhibit at the 1906 Agricultural Hall Show in Islington, London. All that was on the Pickering stand when the exhibition opened was the body for the bus, but the chassis did arrive in time for the two to be married before the show closed. This bus had a four-cylinder Pickering engine of 35-40hp 'which develops its power at 750rpm'. Unusual features included a dual ignition system, Pickering patented wheels with a fixed centre flange, and steering-mounted controls for throttle, air and both ignition systems. The engine drove through a metal to leather clutch and then 'via a telescopic link' to a three-speed gearbox.

Pierce-Arrow

Quality American car maker Pierce-Arrow added trucks to its range in 1910 and later PSVs as well. British ideas, such as worm drive, were incorporated in some of its early commercials as a result of employing engineers from Dennis and Hallford. From 1924 there was a normal-control bus chassis, the model Z. It had a six-cylinder engine as used in the cars and was available in the UK for a time. With a list price of £1,000 it was the most expensive chassis on the market.

Prunel

Another French maker, based near Paris, Prunel built cars and commercial vehicles for just four or five years. A double-decker on a three-ton chassis with 30-33hp four-cylinder engine had a body built by T. H. Lewis of Chalk Farm, London. The body was shipped to France and fitted in the factory. The complete vehicle with invited observers was then driven the 180 miles from Paris to Boulogne in 15hr running time. It then crossed the Channel by ship and covered the 72 miles from Folkestone to London in six hours, all without mishap. The bus was then shown at the 1906 Agricultural Hall Show in Islington.

Ransomes

Better known as a pioneer trolleybus maker, Ransomes, Sims & Jefferies built one battery-electric bus in 1921. It was constructed around a lorry chassis and sold to a colliery in Accrington, Lancashire, to provide works transport.

Regent

Very little appears to be known about the 24hp Regent chassis built in 1905 for omnibus or lorry work and which was demonstrated to the press that year. One noteworthy feature was the use of a single lever 'to operate all the gears, the speeds being placed in consecutive order, with the high speed at the rear of the box'. There were four forward speeds, and the gearbox was mounted immediately ahead of the rear wheels. Applying the handbrake 'put the motor out of gear,' it was said.

Renault

For many years a distinctive feature of numerous Renault models was their unusual bonnet shape, like an upturned coal scuttle. Austin of England used a similar bonnet for some years. By the 1920s the French maker had developed a huge range, from cars to heavy trucks, specialised vehicles to cross the Sahara desert, PSVs and railcars. From the late 1920s there was a range of normal and forward-control coaches, capable of considerable speed. Sir Henry Seagrave demonstrated them in Britain, where a number were sold. Earlier, there had been UK customers for smaller vehicles. For example, Blue Bird Motors of Cwm bought a 26-seat bus in 1925 for its service to Ebbw Vale. The vehicles had a coal-scuttle bonnet, pneumatic tyres at the front and servo-assisted four-wheel brakes — the latter a rarity at that time. Even more impressive were two 1928 45hp six-cylinder normal-control Renaults supplied to John Lee & Son (Rothbury) and Geo Longstaff & Sons (Morpeth). Both were fitted with Strachan & Brown bodies and both worked services into Newcastle. The chassis had extremely long wheelbases, long coal-scuttle bonnets and servo-operated brakes on all wheels; the latter were no doubt essential given the top speed of over 60mph.

Above:
The first — and perhaps only — Regent chassis is demonstrated to the press on a steep hill in Hampstead. Note the early trade plate displayed. *Author's Collection*

Below:
The so-called coal-scuttle bonnet style was a distinctive feature of Renaults for many years. This one dates from 1922. *Author's Collection*

Reo

One of America's better-known makes is Reo, which in the 1920s became the most successful US chassis sold in the UK; the Reo Speed Wagon was particularly popular. Reo had been started by one R. E. Olds in 1904 after what would now be called a boardroom split or coup, in which he was ousted from his very successful Olds Motor Works. That company became Oldsmobile and a major part of General Motors. Olds himself went on to make a success of his second company, Reo, which makes him unique among motoring pioneers.

Reo, like Olds Motor Works, also built cars, having first added commercial vehicles in 1908. Speed Wagons were introduced in 1915, with a new range in the mid-1920s. A few World War 1 Reos had come on to the British market, with Harris & Hasell of Bristol handling the first direct imports here in 1922. However, in 1929 there appears to have been a parting of the ways, with the setting up of Reo Motors (Britain) to assemble and sell the chassis whilst Harris & Hasell produced a new marque (the BAT). The latter lasted less than three years, whereas Reos went on being sold in the UK — albeit in smaller numbers — until 1939.

The first direct imports of Reos into the UK were of small models of little over 1 ton capacity and 27hp four-cylinder engine. Larger models, Sprinters and Pullmans, soon followed with six-cylinder engines and four-wheel brakes. These were officially 'sedan coaches', but four and six-cylinder bus models were also listed. Later, chassis denomination was by letter. Both 20 and 26-seaters were fitted with six-cylinder Gold Crown engines; Reo was unusual among US

Above:
Reos were light and fast, and arguably among the best of the imports; not all US-designed engines withstood fast driving or high mileage. This one, named *Pride of the West*, has a folding canvas roof, but fixed side frames with full-drop windows. Its low build and neat lines give it an imposing appearance. *Arthur Ingram Collection*

makes in building its own engines. The company made much play of this in its sales pitch, particularly with the Silver Crown and Gold Crown engines. The chrome nickel cylinder block of the Gold Crown was said to be seven times harder than the conventional iron blocks used by most makers. With a claimed output of 67bhp at 2,800rpm, aluminium pistons and a seven-bearing crankshaft, the engines contributed to the reputation of high performance, aided by their installation in lightweight chassis.

Several companies that became successful in the coaching field in the late 1920s and early 1930s built themselves up on Reos. Black & White Motorways of Cheltenham began in 1926 with a 14-seat Reo charabanc, acquired as a temporary measure until two 20-seat Reos with London Lorries charabanc bodies could be completed for a new pioneer, Cheltenham-London express service. Seven more Reos were added in the following two years, before the company moved on to Gilfords and Leylands. Yelloway Motor Services bought 12 Reo Major 20-seaters in 1926 and 1927, before acquiring the same number of Reo Pullman 26-seaters in 1928. However, it too moved on to Gilfords and Tilling-Stevens in later years.

Republic

Another American manufacturer to have a degree of success in the UK in the 1920s was Republic, once the largest truck builder in the US. Chassis were conventional, with four-cylinder engines, though drop-frame passenger models were introduced quite early.

Rochet-Schneider

French car maker Rochet-Schneider of Lyon was established well before 1900 and was soon producing trucks and buses fitted with the same engine design. New models from the early 1920s included 1½ and 2½ chassis, the larger having an 18bhp four-cylinder engine. The chassis earned a reputation for durability,

and also for riding quality, enabling the company to build up useful PSV business.

A few chassis were sold in the UK in the 1920s, and the fleet of six charabancs of the Dean Motor Transport Co (taken over by Scottish Motor Traction in 1925) included four of this make.

Below:
The best of both worlds was offered by this Republic exhibited at the 1922 Scottish Motor Show. Called a bus-chara, it could be used as an open charabanc in summer (with cape hood raised if it rained) but the addition of the two-piece detachable top made it an enclosed saloon bus. Two people were said to be able to raise the winter roof, which was in sections, so that a half open, half closed format was also possible.
Author's Collection

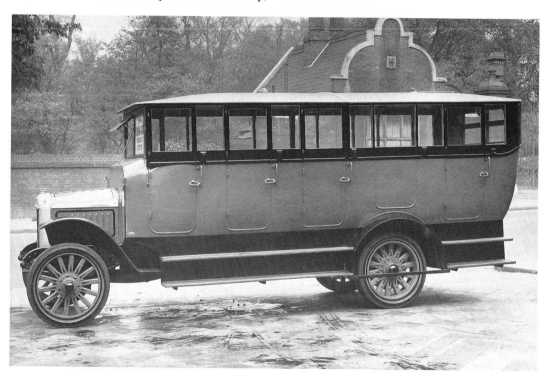

Left:
Republic was early in adopting a low-frame chassis. This one with underslung rear springs and Lycoming engine dates from 1924. Clutch and gearbox are mounted in unit with the engine. *Arthur Ingram Collection*

Romar

A rare make of vehicles indeed, even in its native land, was the Romar, seven of which were bought in late 1915 and early 1916 by the Wellingborough Motor Omnibus Co. All were fitted with new or secondhand open-top double-deck bodies, the latter coming from Leylands in the fleet that had been requisitioned by the military authorities. All the Romars had left the fleet by the end of 1918. Another operator to buy the make was Southdown, which was also seeking replacements for requisitioned buses.

Ryknield Motor Co

This foreign-sounding make was actually built in Burton-upon-Trent, a place better known for its breweries. There was, in fact, brewery interest or backing in Ryknield, with some of its lorries bought by breweries. The first PSV chassis was announced in 1905, and 20 were running in Brussels by 1910. Home operators included Leeds, the LGOC and Todmorden, while Manchester saw both single and double-deckers. The chassis were probably better designed and more solidly built than some other makes. By 1907 an unusual feature was the emergency brake for the conductor. It was operated by a hand wheel at the back of the bus and worked through the driver's handbrake. It applied a pull on a compensating beam and finally transmitted the application to single brake blocks on the exterior of the toothed driving rings which transmitted drive to the rear wheels. These toothed driving rings were no doubt noisy. One imagines this brake system was a result of the Handcross Hill accident to a Milnes-Daimler in 1906. After Ryknield went bankrupt Tom Barton (of what became Barton Transport) was offered some 30 chassis; he bought and resold many, whilst a few entered his own fleet.

St Vincent

This Glasgow maker built small numbers of cars and commercial vehicles up to 1910. They included a charabanc with Aster two-cylinder 14/16hp engine exhibited at the 1908 Edinburgh show; it was described as a 12-seat 'passenger lorry', presumably because the bodywork was detachable.

Saurer

To many people Swiss maker Saurer is best known for its postbuses serving many an Alpine pass. This old-established company sold chassis to the UK over many years, although not in great numbers. The Mersey Railway bought 10 in 1905, some of 24/28hp and others of 28/32hp, fitting all with double-deck bodies. However, a House of Lords decision in 1907 ruled that the railway had no right to run buses and all were sold, six to Kingston upon Hull Corporation.

Another early buyer was another railway, the North Eastern, with six in 1906. They carried single-deck bus or charabanc bodies — bodies were often interchangeable in those days — and ran in many parts of the company's area for many years, one lasting almost 20 years.

But the association with those Alpine passes is appropriate, as Saurer sold successfully in South Wales for two routes over roads previously regarded as too arduous for buses. Following a successful demonstration of a 3AD chassis, South Wales Transport bought seven Brush-bodied 26-seaters to inaugurate its Townhill, Swansea, route in 1926. It was not so much the steepness of the hill, but the length — $1\frac{1}{2}$ miles at an average of 1 in 9.6 with a steepest section of 1 in 5.6 — that caused the problem. The engine had a variable camshaft so it could provide braking downhill, there was a second speed-lock on the gearbox, and a sprag to prevent running backwards. So successful were buses and route that the fleet ultimately totalled 17. However, almost permanent second-gear running gave a ruinous petrol consumption of 3.1mpg, which resulted in AECs and Daimlers (by then improved, though not without engine problems on this work) ousting the last Saurer by 1935.

Independent operator Lewis & James of Newbridge (later to become part of Western Welsh) had either heard about the South Wales' Saurers or J. H. Lewis saw one when he was on holiday in Switzerland, depending on which story you believe. Either way, one was ordered for a new route from Bargoed via Aberbargoed to Markham. This had a half-mile of hill with gradients between 1 in 8 and 1 in 5, with a short length worse at 1 in 4.5. The bus, with a Dodson body, was delivered in September 1926 in the operator's Western & Sirhowy Valley fleetname. However, a bill setting up the West Monmouthshire Omnibus Board, with takeover powers for several routes in its area, had just received the Royal Assent, and the route did not start until June 1927. The so-far unused bus was sold to the board for £1,500 — £250 less than it had cost. So successful was this route (its pence per car mile figure was very high) that soon a second and later a third Saurer were bought by the board. Later, starting in 1930, Leylands replaced the Saurers, and the last of the trio retired in 1939.

Other Saurers used in the UK during the 1920s and 1930s were less colourful.

Scheibler

German maker Scheibler had been building vans and light buses before 1900. From 1903 heavier chassis were offered, and a total of 20 appear to have operated in London during 1907. Their success was, however, shortlived.

Scout

Scout Motors of Salisbury was a small company building cars and commercial vehicles between 1909 and 1921, with a gap from part way through World War 1 until 1920. A number of chassis with chain drive (and later worm drive) were bodied as chara-bancs, while the newly-formed Wilts & Dorset bought five with bus bodies in 1914/15.

Selden

American truck maker Selden was based in Rochester, New York State. In World War 1 it built considerable numbers of 'Liberty' trucks for the US army. Afterwards, the company went on to export in considerable quantities to Europe and Japan. Its range in the early 1920s was relatively simple and standardised, fitted with Continental engines. Continental was a US engine builder which supplied numerous chassis makers. One of the British trade journals at the time said: 'The Selden, like many American truck chassis, lends itself very well to passenger work'.

Below:
The Sentinel-HSG single-decker was shown in chassis form at the Kelvin Hall, Glasgow, show in 1938. The gas producer plant can be seen mounted at the rear. *Ian Allan Library*

Sentinel

The most innovative of the makers of steam road vehicles was Sentinel of Shrewsbury, which built saleable models long after other makers had ceased. However, its one entry into the passenger field, in 1924, was of dated design.

Sentinel-HSG

Sentinel was a maker of steam lorries which, by 1933, had produced relatively advanced designs with shaft drive. However, within a few years, it was anxious, if not desperate, to reduce its dependence on steam and in 1938 bought High Speed Gas (GB). At the motor show that year, in Glasgow's Kelvin Hall, it exhibited a bus chassis with producer gas plant at the rear. The chassis, like the earlier Gilfords (HSG) example, again used a Gilford chassis, but this time with an American Hercules engine. It subsequently gained a Cowieson body and underwent trials at Merthyr Tydfil and in London. At some point during World War 2 the original engine was converted back to petrol.

Shefflex

Shefflex is one of the stranger stories in vehicle building. Sheffield-Simplex of Tinsley (Sheffield) was a luxury car maker which, during World War 1, assembled Commer commercial vehicles under contract. After the contract ended, the company found itself left with quantities of components which were assembled and sold as Shefflex trucks. More problems occurred and, as a result, R. A. Johnstone bought those remaining and apparently had little problem selling them. Encouraged, he restarted production at Tinsley. The company subsequently became Shefflex Motor Co. It began with two goods models, but soon added a 24-seat passenger chassis. By the mid-1930s, if not earlier, refuse vehicles had become the main output.

Shelvoke & Drewry

Harry Shelvoke and James Drewry produced the first S&D Freighter in 1923. They designed it as a low-frame vehicle, easy to drive and able to be driven slowly for use as a dust cart or refuse collection vehicle. It had very small wheels, an engine mounted transversely just ahead of a set-back front axle, and tiller controls for steering and for working the change-speed mechanism of the epicyclic gearbox. Much later, passenger models changed to conventional steering wheels.

In 1924 Bill Gates of Worthing saw the bus potential for a vehicle that was easy for the elderly to board and alight from. His Tramocars fleet led a minor fashion which resulted in some 50 S&Ds being built for PSV use, mainly at seaside resorts such as Blackpool, Bournemouth, Douglas and Exmouth. The final two buses for the Tramocars fleet, delivered in 1938 after it sold out to Southdown, were even more unusual in having the engine mounted transversely behind the back axle.

Sheppee

A retired Indian Army officer, Col H. F. Sheppee had set up the Sheppee Motor Co in York to pursue his enthusiasm for steam-powered road vehicles. As it took him some 10 years to build a total of 14 vehicles, mainly goods chassis, his interest was obviously in design rather than production! It is thought the chassis

may have been from existing vehicles rather than purpose-built. The boilers were liquid fuelled and produced steam at a pressure of 900psi, though no two vehicles were alike. There was a steam charabanc built either before or during 1909.

Above:
The Sheppee was built in York and its minuscule total production included this steam charabanc. Like the more successful Thomas Clarkson, interest in design improvements was uppermost. *Author's Collection*

Simms-Welbeck

The Simms Manufacturing Co of London made mainly electrical components for motor vehicles, continuing with this business up to the time of the Routemaster bus. However, it also produced a few complete motor vehicles which were fitted with its own make of engine. Both van and heavier chassis were built between about 1904 and 1907. A few engines were also supplied to others; the Alexandra (Newport & South Wales) Docks & Railway Co bought two 20/25hp engines for fitting to two 1903 Milnes-Daimler buses it was running. Pioneer London motorbus operator Vanguard (the London Motor Omnibus Co) ran a Simms double-decker which was said to be the only double-decker of this make. A bodied single-decker for the Durham & District Motor Omnibus Co was delivered by road from London in June 1906. The 270-mile journey over two days was covered in a running time of 16hr 52min. Vehicles were known as Simms and Simms-Welbeck.

Singer

Better-remembered as a car maker, Singer occasionally offered van models. However, at the 1929 Commercial Motor Show the company launched a complete range of commercial vehicles under the title Singer Industrial Motors. These had nothing in common with the cars. A 3.1 litre four-cylinder engine developing 60hp, with five-bearing crankshaft, servo-assisted four-wheel brakes and twin rear wheels were standard. In 1930/31 the chassis was described as low-loading, and was available as a normal-control 20-seat PSV.

Spa

An apparently short name represented the initials of a long one; Spa chassis were built in Italy by Societa Ligure Piemontese Automobili of Turin. Established in 1908, the company soon developed a whole range of commercial vehicles. By 1923 there were also two passenger-carrying models, the smaller — a 20-seater — boasting such refinements as pneumatic tyres and an electric starter motor. A bank failure two years later took the company into the hands of Fiat, with Fiat (England) offering both makes for goods and passenger-carrying for some years. It was not until 1947 that Spa was finally absorbed by Fiat.

In Britain, the Royal Agricultural Show was an unlikely but popular venue for both truck and bus exhibits, and the 1928 Show saw Fiat (England) showing three Fiat trucks, one Spa truck and one Spa bus. The bus had a 52bhp four-cylinder engine and a 24-seat bus body.

Star

Star had been making bicycles for some years prior to 1900, later moved on to cars and before World War 1 had commercial vehicles and a charabanc chassis in its range. After the war it produced medium capacity goods and passenger chassis that were relatively light yet well made — and fast. Probably they were too well made, and thus expensive, for the highly competitive markets of the late 1920s. Guy bought the company in 1928 and moved production to a new factory, still in Wolverhampton, but by 1932 it was all over.

Relatively late in its life Star produced a low-frame 20-seat passenger chassis, and from it developed its Star Flyer. This was fitted with a 3.2 litre, six-cylinder, overhead-valve engine fitted with seven bearings. There was a spiral bevel rear axle, excellent suspension — and a laden top speed of well over

50mph. A neat touch, and one which exemplified the hand-building of the marque, was the casting of stars on components such as petrol filler cap, front axle and differential cover. Guy is said to have handed (or perhaps sold) the design of the Star Flyer to AJS, which built it as the AJS Pilot. Guy itself bodied at least one Flyer.

Scottish Motor Traction was an enthusiastic user, buying 38 in 1928 and fitting them with 20-seat bus or 14-seat coach bodies. The last was withdrawn in 1936.

Below:
A strange purchase, one might have thought, was this Star charabanc acquired new by the Royal Naval Air Service in 1916. Note the high fleet number. *Author's Collection*

Bottom:
A much later Star is this 1928 model, one of a large batch for SMT which received either 14-seat coach bodies or 20-seat bus bodies. *Ian Allan Library*

Stewart

US truck and bus maker Stewart had a Canadian assembly plant in the 1930s and exported chassis to Europe. However, it ceased to offer its US-built 20-seater in the UK after about 1931. Two Stewarts were exhibited at the 1929 Commercial Motor Show, both with six-cylinder engines. One had a body by Newns.

Stirling and Scott-Stirling

With advertisements in the technical press in 1906 claiming an annual production of 500 buses, Scott-Stirling could have been thought to be the country's biggest bus builder. But it was not true and by 1908 the company had gone.

Stirling had been an early maker, based in Hamilton, and ran its own-assembled wagonettes with Daimler engines as buses in Stirling. It also built three 14-seaters for the North Eastern Railway in 1903. Later, buses — now known as Scott-Stirlings — were assembled at Twickenham, Middlesex. After a few single-deckers, production turned to double-deckers, in which the driver sat high with the engine beneath and ahead of his feet. By March 1907 the London Power Omnibus (fleetname Pioneer) was running 62 of the type, but making losses of 7d (3p) a mile. By July Pioneer went bankrupt and vanished. The availability of all these secondhand buses also unsettled the whole new bus market.

Straker-Squire

Sidney Straker was an engineer of considerable talent. In 1900, as consulting engineer to Daimler of Coventry, he designed the first Daimler multi-passenger vehicle, a small charabanc. He lived in London, but had interests in Bristol with the engineering company Owen, Brazil & Holborow. His association with the firm began in 1899, and two years later the Straker Steam Vehicle Co was formed. It built steam vehicles, including two double-deckers for the British Electric Traction Group in 1901, a single-decker in 1903 for a service to Stratford-upon-Avon, and also petrol-engined vehicles.

At about the time the firm arranged to sell German-built Bussings in Britain it was renamed Sidney Straker & Squire, and soon had to move to a larger factory in Bristol to cope with demand. By the time the three major London motorbus operators combined in 1908 (into the LGOC), they were operating 261 Straker-Squires. The maker gradually introduced UK-sourced components into its product and at the same time introduced its own designs.

After World War 1 ended the company moved to the London area, announcing a new design with its 'A'-type. This had a four-cylinder monobloc engine of 55bhp, four-speed gearbox and worm drive, and — unusually — was of semi-forward-control layout. It was a fast vehicle and in the early days of pirate (or independent) bus operation in London proved popular since it could easily outpace the slow and lumbering

Above:
Many tram operators were quick to spot the potential of the motorbus. The quaintly-named Gateshead Tramways Motor Service took delivery of these two Straker-Squires with unusual front entrances. Note the single offside headlights and the headgear of the drivers and their assistants. *Author's Collection*

Below:
By the time this Dodson-bodied Straker-Squire was delivered in 1911, the chassis maker was claiming that it was built 'mainly of British components'. The Brighton, Hove & Preston United Omnibus Co had been formed in 1884 and had begun trials with motor-buses as early as 1902. In 1915 the BHPU sold its Brighton-Worthing service, for which this bus is lettered, to the new Southdown Motor Services. *Author's Collection*

AECs of the LGOC. At this stage Straker-Squire also offered its own bodywork and the availability of this complete 'package' built to the stringent requirements of the Metropolitan Police was a further attraction to newcomers.

The quick acceleration and speed were never matched by reliability, unfortunately, and the company went into receivership first in 1925 and again in 1926.

Studebaker

Studebaker is probably best remembered for its large cars in the UK, but this old-established business built horse-drawn vehicles for many years followed by electric ones. Cars and petrol-engined commercial chassis followed later, and by the mid-1920s there was a range of normal-control chassis powered by a 5.9 litre six-cylinder engine used in the cars. Later the range of PSVs went from 14-seaters to large single-

deckers with eight-cylinder petrol engines. A few found their way to the UK, and the early fleet of Black & White Motorways included four, built between 1927 and 1929; all were 20-seaters. Clan Motorways had eight, with 14, 20 or 24-seat bodies running on its express services from Glasgow in 1928.

Sunbeam (SMC)

Sunbeam was a car maker and, like many others, desperately looking for diversification in the hard times of the late 1920s. Buses and coaches seemed to offer hope and in 1929 the company produced the Pathan four-wheeler and Sikh six-wheeler. Both were beautifully engineered (and expensive) and most had an engine of nearly eight litres with a seven-bearing crankshaft, dry sump lubrication and other innovations perhaps inspired by previous experience building aero engines.

Right:
Sunbeams were beautifully engineered, and their double-decker six-wheelers were impressive looking vehicles. But only two were sold. This was the second, which entered service with London independent Westminster Omnibus in 1933. It was fitted with a 64-seat Dodson body. By this time the Metropolitan Police allowed windscreens, but Westminster's managing director did not approve of them. *Ian Allan Library*

Just two of the six-wheelers were sold, though ultimate conversion of a third, unsold, chassis to a trolleybus opened up a new and much more successful field.

Pathans sold rather better as single-deck coaches. Rootes bought the struggling company in 1935 and subsequently two AEC directors joined its board for a time. There followed a single AEC Regent double-decker with Gardner engine and Sunbeam radiator grille; but no other motorbuses or coaches were offered.

Talbot

Better-known for its cars, Clement Talbot built vans, trucks, ambulances and coaches at various times between 1914 and 1938. A 20-seat coach chassis was first introduced soon after World War 1. This was of conventional normal-control layout. Highland Motorways ran a Glasgow-Inverness service in 1928 with Talbots claimed to seat 26. The Rootes Group took over the company in 1935, the same year it bought Sunbeam.

Thames Ironworks

Thames Ironworks was an old-established shipbuilder in southeast London, which diversified into road vehicles. Its first bus chassis was built in 1905 and a year later offered what was claimed to be the first PSV with six-cylinder engine. Charabancs were apparently made in reasonable numbers, but the company is best remembered for its final vehicle, which could have been mistaken for its first. It looked like a horse-drawn stagecoach without the horses, and was a semi-forward-control double-decker. Amazingly, one of these vehicles survives in the National Motor

Museum. It was built in 1913, the last year of the company's existence. An earlier user was pioneer operator J. W. Cann's London & South Coast Motor Services of Folkestone, which bought eight, the first few in 1906. However, some of the earliest vehicles lasted barely a year in the fleet.

Thornycroft

John I. Thornycroft & Co was a builder of steam launches, based by the River Thames at Chiswick. It added vehicle building to its products after one of its lightweight vertical steam engines was fitted to a van in 1896. Within two years a move to larger premises at Basingstoke was necessary to meet demand.

The rather bizarre roofed double-decker steam bus that operated briefly in London during 1902 has attracted a disproportionate amount of attention; in the same year the Belfast & Northern Counties Railway put into service in Belfast two similar buses, but fitted with 14-seat single-deck bodies. They ran for at least six years — before being replaced by horsebuses, but the chassis were converted to lorries, one of which worked until 1925. The railway, which by now had become the Midland Railway (Northern Counties Committee), bought two more Thornycrofts in 1905, this time petrol-engined charabancs for summer excursions.

From 1902 the company had been building paraffin and petrol-engined lorries and by 1905 it had a considerable range of petrol vehicles available in the UK. Two-cylinder 16hp or four-cylinder 30hp engines were later offered for passenger chassis seating up to 34. The famous 'J'-type was first built in 1913; during World War 1 some 5,000 were built, with more following after the war. Not all wartime ones went for military service; the Great North of

Left:
This early Thornycroft 'motor chara-banc' was operated by the Lake District Road Traffic Co and, when photographed, had been in the fleet for eight years. No doubt it was running on gas because of World War 1 fuel shortages. *Author's Collection*

Centre left:
Phoenix Motor & Omnibus Co was a one-bus London independent operator, which began with this Thornycroft 'J' early in 1924. The business and bus were sold in 1927. The bus had a standard London-style Dodson body, and the chassis too had to meet the stringent requirements of Scotland Yard on turning circle and other details. *Author's Collection*

Below:
Thornycroft had considerable success with sales to the Isle of Man in the late 1920s, supplying 46 buses in three years. Among the last was this 1929 BC Forward with Hall Lewis 28-seat body. However, there were no more bus sales to the island. *Author's Collection*

Above:
The Great Western Railway bought large numbers of Thornycrofts for passenger and for goods use. This 1925 A1 with Vickers 19-seat bus body ultimately passed to Western National. *Author's Collection*

Above right:
Southampton Corporation bought a number of Thornycroft Daring double-deckers in the early 1930s. This one, new in 1934, was unique in being delivered with an AEC six-cylinder diesel engine; earlier Darings in the fleet were petrol-engined, whilst later ones were fitted with Gardner diesel engines. *Rex Kennedy Collection*

Scotland Railway bought three from Basingstoke and fitted its own bus bodies in 1915/16. The 'J' became a popular choice for PSVs after the war. Scottish Motor Traction bought some 50 ex-WD chassis between 1920 and 1924, overhauled them and lengthened the chassis by 12in (300mm) before fitting new 27-seat charabanc or 28-seat bus bodies. Portsmouth Corporation Tramways bought 10 'Js' in 1919, fitting open-top double-deck bodies to them; one still survives.

A particularly successful model was the 1½ ton A1 introduced in 1924. Over 1,000 were said to have gone into service by the end of 1925. They had the gearbox in unit with the engine, and were also offered as 20-seat bus chassis. Later there was the larger A2 as well. A much bigger chassis was the Lightning coach of 1927, 'a surprise to all our competitors,' said Thornycroft. Its 70bhp side-valve six-cylinder engine had 'wet liners for the cylinder block, two detachable heads, a camshaft driven from the rear end of the crankshaft, seven main bearings and full pressure lubrication'. It was said to be capable of 50mph fully laden, so it was as well it had servo-brakes on all four

wheels. It was of normal-control layout, with seats for up to 26.

Unit construction for the engine, clutch and gearbox was soon extended to larger vehicles, and chassis frames were lowered between the axles.

Railway business was good in the late 1920s. The Great North of Scotland Railway had bought more 'J'-types in 1919 and again in 1921; its successor, the London & North Eastern Railway, bought a batch of 38 32-seat Thornycroft 'BCs' in 1928/29. The Isle of Man Railway was another success, with 22 buses, nearly all 'BCs', supplied in 1928; these followed 19 'A2s' in 1927 which went mainly to companies in which the railway had an interest. Subsequently the vehicles operated with the railway-owned Isle of Man Road Services. But jewel in the crown was the Great Western Railway, which also bought numerous Thornycroft goods vehicles. It bought 40 'A1s' with 19-seat bodies in 1925 and returned to the make in 1928 for 15 'A1s' and six others. In 1929 five 'A1s', 12 'A2s' and 11 'BCs' were acquired. The 'BCs' seated 26 or 32. Virtually all the GWR and LNER-owned vehicles passed to the bus companies in which the railways had bought a financial stake and so there were no more railway orders, and precious few from the bus companies.

During the 1930s it was probably the export side that kept the bus business afloat. The years 1930 and 1931 must have been poor for sales, but at the 1931 Olympia Show the company launched two new models and had two or three of each bodied as demonstrators. These were the Daring double-decker and the Cygnet single-decker. Older, fairly dated designs had sold at the rate of four or five a year, so seven Darings for 1932 was a slight improvement, but just 14 Cygnets sold was a poor result. Petrol-engined Cygnets were said to be very thirsty.

By 1934 Thornycroft was offering its own diesel

engine, a 7.88 litre six-cylinder direct injection unit. Two buses so fitted went to the Stalybridge, Hyde, Mossley & Dukinfield Joint Board and two more to Southampton Corporation. However, the SHMD examples soon gained Gardner engines. SHMD was the company's biggest supporter, with more than 80 Thornycrofts in its fleet at one stage. Its manager, incidentally, was a former employee! SHMD bought its last Darings in 1936, while Southampton took a total of four in 1936/37 with Gardner 5LW engines. These were the last double-deckers built. Some of the Southampton ones were sold to Nottingham for further service in 1946 and lasted until 1948, so they cannot have been that bad. Certainly they were far better than the four-cylinder 'LC-DD', four of which were bought by Cardiff Corporation in 1930 — their brakes were said to need adjusting three times a day, though their mechanical performance was improved by 1934 when Gardner 6LW engines were fitted.

The problem in the mid-1930s was, of course, that the opposition had improved its product by leaps and bounds and was selling in sufficient numbers to support research and development — unlike Thornycroft.

There were also some smaller models offered in the 1930s. There was a lightweight Ardent 20-seater and subsequently a Dainty. Later, the Sturdy, a low-weight, high capacity truck, was also offered as a 26-seater called the Beautyride. By 1939, this was the only PSV still listed.

Tilling-Stevens and TSM

Early motorbuses were heavy, primitive machines, difficult to drive. Those who did drive them could often unwittingly cause considerable damage to frail gearboxes and other components. This led London operator Thomas Tilling to experiment with a petrol-electric. Three men designed it: the engineer and

manager of Tilling's motor department, Percy Frost Smith; Frank Brown, chairman of David Brown & Sons of Huddersfield, which manufactured the final drive; and W. A. Stevens, managing director of W. A. Stevens of Maidstone, which designed the electric transmission and assembled. The bus was generally known as the SB&S. Surprisingly, J. & E. Hall of Dartford, builders of the Hallford, whose chassis was used as the base got no mention.

The petrol engine drove a dynamo, which in turn fed current to two electric motors, each placed outside the main frame and each driving one rear wheel via a carden shaft. This bus entered service in London in 1908; it was known to the Tilling crews as 'Queenie' because it behaved so well. It ran some 60,000 miles, during which various improvements were made. An improved version was sold in small numbers as Hallford-Stevens but Tilling did not buy any.

Instead it developed the Tilling-Stevens petrol-electric, which it built in its own workshops in Bull Yard, Peckham, London using electrical equipment from W. A. Stevens. The first model was the TTA1, production of which started in 1911. The following year Tilling bought control of W. A. Stevens and by the time production of this model ended in 1914, it was running 174 of them. A few had also been sold to other operators. A distinctive feature of the TTA1 was the Renault-style bonnet; the radiator was mounted behind the engine because it would not be so exposed to road dirt. The 30hp four-cylinder engine drove a 20kW dynamo and, unlike the SB&S, there was just one motor, which powered a worm and wheel live back axle via a short propshaft. The chassis frame was of pressed steel, and varied in depth.

One unforeseen advantage of the Tilling-Stevens was that it was of no interest to the military, whereas the authorities commandeered huge numbers of 'B'-types and Daimlers among others.

The postwar AEC 'K'-type with 46-seat body was

Left:
This example of the first production petrol-electric (model TTA1) was one of two hired by Thomas Tilling to the Great Eastern Railway in the summer of 1914 for use on a new Dovercourt-Harwich service. Other TTA1s were, of course, sold to outside operators. *Author's Collection*

Right:
Later petrol-electric models were of more conventional appearance. This demonstrator dates from 1921 and was one of the postwar improved TS3A type, with seats for 48. *Author's Collection*

Centre right:
Photographed on Brighton's seafront in postwar years, this conventional Tilling-Stevens B9B had been new to Southdown in 1927, and gained a new Harrington body in 1934, at which time the chassis may have been updated. Sold in 1938, it was later bought by Unique Coaches (Brighton) and lasted until 1954. *Author's Collection*

Below:
Despite the introduction of a new double-deck model in 1931 with six-cylinder engine, few double-deckers were sold in the 1930s. However, in 1933 the newly-formed Benfleet & District Motor Services of Benfleet, near Southend, bought three D60A6 chassis with Park Royal bodies. At least one later acquired an AEC 8.8 litre diesel engine. Benfleet & District was later taken over by Westcliff-on-Sea Motor Services, which subsequently became part of Eastern National. *Ian Allan Library*

on London's streets in numbers before the first TS3As, with their 48-seat bodies, entered service there in 1921. The TS3As had the driver alongside the engine. The TS3 had been put into production earlier, and the TS7 followed in 1923. However, these and later designs were mechanically and electrically little changed, although radiators were now at the front.

The chassis sold to many operators, apart from Tilling's own business; Wolverhampton Corporation was one sizeable user. The company began to make conventional petrol chassis too in 1919, and in 1926 introduced the B9 low-frame Express single-deckers. They were offered in normal and forward-control forms and sold well, as did the succeeding B10. However, the company also persevered with petrol-electrics, producing two new models (a four-wheeler and a six-wheeler) in 1929 which attracted little interest.

Thomas Tilling tried one of the new petrol-electrics (a TS17A) with special light alloy frame (to reduce weight) and its own body, and then a couple more, plus an early AEC Regent in London and Brighton, and a Leyland Titan and a Daimler CF6 in Brighton only. It then returned the TS17A chassis to Tilling-Stevens and went out and ordered almost 300 Regents, and followed this by disposing of its shareholding in Tilling-Stevens. It was all very odd. Why had Tilling's subsidiary been allowed to persist with an outdated double-deck design, with a relatively high chassis, for so long? Was, perhaps, Tilling management more interested in buying and running bus businesses?

The new company badged its chassis TSM and developed further conventional models, later offering Gardner diesel engines as an option. But sales fell drastically, particularly after the Bristol bus building business came into the Tilling fold.

Two surprises in 1937 were the purchase of the ailing Vulcan of Southport (mainly for its truck models) and the appearance at the Motor Show of two three-axle chassis with underfloor engines and seven-speed pre-selector gearboxes. Known as the Successor, the model had horizontally-opposed diesel engines of 7.45 litre; one was shown in chassis form, the other with an elegant Duple coach body. Probably neither ran for an operator.

The company also changed name back to Tilling-Stevens and its fortunes were subsequently helped by a revival in interest in petrol-electric chassis for use as mobile searchlights in World War 2.

Traffic

The American-built Traffic was a fairly conventional normal-control chassis, of which a few were used in the UK as buses a year or so after the end of World War 1.

Turgan

This French maker changed from cars to commercials, and from steam power to petrol. A steam double-decker was built in 1900 and in 1906 just one petrol-engined double-decker began running in London between Oxford Circus and Streatham Common. Turgan ceased trading in 1907.

Unic

French maker Unic is best remembered in the British market for its taxis, some of which could still be found working in London during the 1950s, though of venerable age. Vans and light goods vehicles were also sold here for many years, but the 1920s saw passenger chassis of smaller size also on offer. For example, the Scottish Motor Show of 1922 saw goods

vehicles from about ³/₄ ton to 1¹/₂ ton, with a passenger version based on the 1 ton goods model. It had pneumatic tyres all round and a coach body with seats for 14. There was a four-speed gearbox and a leather cone clutch. Tobin of Margate, an operator acquired by East Kent Road Car, had bought mainly Unic 14 or 17-seat charabancs between 1922 and 1927, having a total of 12; he traded under the fleet-name of 'Unique'! PSVs were last listed in the UK in 1932, when 14, 20 and 28-seaters were offered.

Vulcan

Any long-serving employee of Vulcan would have felt no stranger to financial crises and management reorganisations, for these were numerous over the life of the company, which, nevertheless, survived a long time. Vulcan began, like so many, making cars. Thomas and Joseph Hampson were brothers who outgrew their Southport premises twice within a few years, then moving to nearby Crossens, reforming the business at the same time to the Vulcan Motor & Engineering Co. Wartime saw production of just commercial vehicles, but problems in 1919 resulted in both brothers leaving. Not long after, Vulcan joined the unsuccessful Harper-Bean consortium, which was also shortlived. There was another reorganisation in 1928, but by 1931 the company was in the hands of the receiver. Production continued and in 1938 the factory was sold to a trailer maker whilst Tilling-Stevens took over the assets and goodwill, transferring production to its Maidstone factory under the new name of Vulcan Motors.

The first acknowledged passenger version of Vulcan chassis came in 1926 as 20- and 26-seat models of conventional layout. After that there were almost bewildering annual changes with larger chassis being added: a 30-seater in 1928, 32 and 36-seaters in 1929, and even a 53-seat double-decker (the Emperor) in 1930. By this date the models were named; Countess, Duke, Duchess, Prince and Princess were all single-deckers. Forward-control layout was standard on some models, six-cylinder petrol engines

came in — initially on the 20-seater in 1928 — but it all became somewhat chaotic, at least to the outsider, with no passenger models being listed in one or two years, and then several the next.

The truth was, no doubt, that things were pretty desperate, and probably almost anything would have been built at the right price for a purchaser with cash in hand. One remarkable success, or dramatic failure depending on how you look at it, was the order from Glasgow Corporation for 25 Emperors, delivered in 1931/32. They joined a fleet that was already running numbers of (very satisfactory) Leyland Titans and AEC Regents, alongside which the Vulcans were a considerable disappointment. One can only assume that the transport committee selected Emperors because of their low price. Within three or four years Glasgow had fitted Leyland radiators and engines to most, but by 1940 they had all been scrapped. Even before that date their public appearances in service seem to have been rare.

In a year when Vulcan (in theory) offered no passenger models, it built a couple for Douglas Corporation. They were small-wheel forward-control models on which Vulcan-built bodywork was mounted. They were designed to meet the requirements of the Douglas general manager for a pair of summer runabouts, with an open-sided toastrack layout on the nearside. A long folding and windowed door design stayed, concertina-like, at the rear in fine weather but, if it rained, it could be slid forward to keep the passengers dry. Three similar bodies were also produced by Vulcan for use on Douglas horse-trams.

W & G

The full name of this company was W. & G. du Cros. It was based at Acton in London and its diverse production included ambulances, PSVs and refuse collection vehicles. The last-named were usually badged du Cros, presumably to avoid associating anything so mundane with passenger-carrying vehicles. The mid-1920s saw the company offer goods and charabanc chassis, with a fast, low-frame six-cylinder bus introduced in 1926, and later forward-control models were added. Passenger chassis sold well for a time, but faded rapidly and production ceased in the early 1930s, although chassis were still listed in buyers' guides up to 1936. Most vehicles went to smaller operators, but there was a 'Corporation' model bus, as W & G called it. This was a long, normal-control vehicle. Bournemouth Corporation, then running mainly trams, bought 15 of the type with front entrances for one-man operation.

Walker

Walkers were probably the most successful battery-electric trucks built in the USA. A number were exported to the UK. Just one appears to have been bodied as a bus, in 1921. It was bought by Liverpool Corporation, which also built the 25-seat body. It was used to carry children between their homes and a special school.

Wallace

One of the more imaginative entrants to the market after World War 1 was the Wallace, produced by Richmond Motor Lorries of Shepherd's Bush, London. S. A. Wallace had been chief engineer of AEC and began importing a selection of components from US makers for assembly in the UK (rather than a complete model in component form). The main components were the Continental Red Seal four-cylinder engine, a three-speed gearbox and a bevel-drive rear axle.

Trucks and charabancs were offered, but assembly ended in 1922. At least one Wallace was bodied as a single-deck bus, while White Motors Service on the Isle of Man had an 18-seat charabanc on pneumatic tyres.

Ward La France

American maker Ward La France is best-known for its fire appliances, though it also built truck chassis. Production was on a surprisingly small scale, using bought-in parts throughout. Pneumatic tyres were offered from an early stage.

One Ward La France operated in South Wales for some years. It was owned by E. E. (Ernie) Snow, an enterprising and inventive operator who built up a fleet of luxurious charabancs after World War 1. This Ward La France had hood and door mechanisms of Snow's own design, and a 10-note organ that was used to wake sleeping residents when the charabanc returned from excursions.

Watson

Henry Watson & Sons of Newcastle-upon-Tyne was an engineering concern producing castings. It had also assembled the British Berna. Then, after World War 1, the company announced its own product, a $3^1/2$-$4^1/2$ ton bonneted truck with four-cylinder engine. Engine and gearbox were mounted in a subframe which ran inside the longitudinal chassis frame. A passenger-carrying derivative was subsequently offered, with a bigger engine. Production petered out some time in the late 1920s.

THIS ILLUSTRATION SHOWS OUR "CORPORATION" MODEL BUS, AS SUPPLIED TO THE BOURNEMOUTH CORPORATION TRAMWAYS DEPT., AND IS BUT ONE OF NUMEROUS TYPES WE HAVE SUPPLIED TO PROMINENT UNDERTAKINGS IN ALL PARTS OF THE COUNTRY. LET US QUOTE YOU FOR YOUR REQUIREMENTS.

WRITE FOR CATALOGUE NOW.

OUR RANGE OF MODELS INCLUDE :—
30 CWTS., 2-TON AND 2½-3 TON—COMMERCIAL—20, 26, 30, 32 AND 36 SEATERS—PASSENGER.

W. & G. DU CROS, LTD.
177, THE VALE, ACTON, LONDON, W.3.
Phone: CHISWICK 0800.

Left: Advertising by W & G in the late 1920s made much of its order for Bournemouth Corporation. Bournemouth used them on feeder services to its trams, but its next order went to Karrier. *Author's Collection*

White

One of the best known, longest-lived and most successful makers in the USA was White. It originated as the White Sewing Machine Co, of Cleveland, but retitled itself without the sewing machine part of its name in 1906, by which time it was already building steam trucks and vans as well as cars. Petrol-engined cars followed a few years later, then trucks and by 1918 buses too. Few of its products found their way to the UK, but United Automobile Services bought a number from the United States Army in France after World War 1. They had pneumatic tyres, seated about 20 and were left-hand drive. They were fast, and used as 'chasers' on routes where there was competition.

Willys-Overland and Willys-Knight

Willys-Overland was a long-established American truck maker. It had links with other makers and with car manufacturers. At one time there was a UK branch of Willys-Overland in Stockport, which in the 1920s sold a one-ton chassis based on the Overland Four Car. In the late 1920s Willys-Overland built an export PSV chassis known as the Willys-Knight, with a six-cylinder sleeve-valve engine of this make. Willys Overland Crossley, a company jointly owned with Crossley, later assembled Willys-Overland chassis in the UK.

A few Willys-Overlands and Willys-Knights operated in the UK, usually with smaller operators. In the mid-1930s Western National Omnibus Co and Southern National took over a number from local operators selling out. Some of them had locally-built Mumford bodies seating 14 or 18. There were various others, loosely described as Willys, that seated between 14 and 20.

Wolseley and Wolseley-Siddeley

If Frank Searle had not persuaded the LGOC to build his design of bus chassis, the company would have placed a large order for Wolseley-Siddeley chassis, of which there were already 90 in the fleet. From 1901 to 1905 Wolseley's remarkable range of products, which included cars, vans, trucks, buses and fire appliances, was masterminded by general manager Herbert Austin, who then went off to start his own company.

Following Austin's departure, the vehicles became known as Wolseley-Siddeleys as J. D. Siddeley took over Austin's position. A single petrol-electric bus was built in 1907, the engine driving a BTH electric

Below:
The original Wolseleys had two-cylinder horizontal engines but later models were more substantially built, with a four-cylinder vertical engine. The biggest fleet running them was that of the LGOC. Note the short-working board displayed at the bottom of the side windows: it reads 'Oxford Circus Only this journey'.
Author's Collection

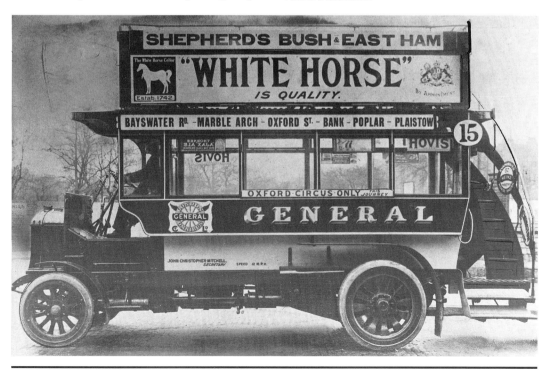

Above:
A 1906 Wolseley bus chassis, photographed from the same angle as the bodied bus. The position of the engine beneath the driver's feet is clearly seen. Note the shaft drive from the engine to the final drive of twin chains; the original design had side chain drive throughout. *Author's Collection*

motor on each rear wheel. The Great Western Railway was an early user of Wolseleys, but in 1906 returned one to the maker as unsatisfactory, taking in part exchange two new ones similar to those running in London. Three more similar vehicles were subsequently acquired; all five were double-deckers. Wolseley's one-ton chassis was often sold as a charabanc. True bus building appears to have ceased before World War 1, though truck production continued. Ultimately all commercial vehicle production ceased. Later Morris acquired Wolseley and built Morris Commercials in the factory.

Yellow Coach

Chicago-based Yellow Coach Manufacturing was formed in 1923 as a subsidiary of a bus company. It was the idea of John D. Hertz, a car salesman who earlier developed a special design of car for sale as a taxi. Thousands of his Yellow Cabs were built and sold. Subsequently he bought control of Chicago Motor Bus and its bus building subsidiary, American Motor Bus Co, and joined them with Fifth Avenue Coach Co of New York. In addition, a new factory was provided.

Key personnel included George Alan Green, who became vice-president of Yellow Coach. He had worked for Vanguard in London, left, but subsequently became chief assistant engineer of the LGOC under Frank Searle. Green then went to America, becoming general manager of Fifth Avenue, and was responsible for the design of its open-top double-deckers. Green had a flair for what today would be called marketing, and saw a need for three reliable and durable types of vehicle: a 29-passenger city bus (Yellow Coach Type Z), a more comfortable 25-29 seater for longer distances (Type Y), and a 17-21 seater for feeder services and for premium-fare express work (Type X). Yellow Coach was later to pioneer the transverse rear engine with angle drive. General Motors bought control of the company in

1925, subsequently merging it with its own operation.

The LGOC had always kept an eye on US developments, even sending teams on study tours from time to time, and bought two Yellow Coaches. It put a 'Z'-type, complete with a Chiswick-built 25-seat coach body, into service in 1925 and the following year added an 'X'-type with its own 11-seat body. Both coaches went into the private hire department. The 'Z'-type had a four-cylinder Silent Knight sleeve-valve engine made by an Illinois company (which was later acquired by Hertz) under licence from Daimler in Coventry.

Another key member of Yellow Coach not so far mentioned was George J. Rackham, its chief engineer for three years. He had worked with Vanguard, was later the LGOC's chief draughtsman and had followed Green to the States. He later came back to the UK to design Leyland's legendary Titan, before moving to AEC to design Regals, Regents and Renowns.

Yorkshire

One of the better known builders of steam lorries was the Yorkshire company. It had a patented boiler mounted transversely over the front axle. In 1917 the Yorkshire Patent Steam Wagon Co built one steam bus in its Hunslet, Leeds, works for Provincial Tramways Co of Grimsby. After being used as a single-deck bus for two years it became a lorry for the operator.

Crossley's first true passenger models were single-deckers aimed at the market in general, but later its interests moved to chassis for the municipal market. *Author's Collection*

HERBERT E. TAYLOR & CO
CRINGLEFORD
NORWICH.

EATON COACHWO...

Crossley